THE CHRIST OF
Christmas

THE CHRIST OF
Christmas

JAMES MONTGOMERY BOICE

P&R
PUBLISHING
P.O. BOX 817 • PHILLIPSBURG • NEW JERSEY 08865-0817

©2009 by Linda M. Boice

Previously issued 1983 Moody Press.
Reissued 2009 by P&R Publishing.

Unless otherwise indicated, all Scripture quotations are from the HOLY BIBLE, NEW INTERNATIONAL VERSION®. NIV®. Copyright © 1973, 1978, 1984 by International Bible Society. Used by permission of Zondervan Publishing House. All rights reserved.

Italics within Scripture quotations indicate emphasis added.

Printed in Canada

The Library of Congress has catalogued the hardcover edition as follows:

Boice, James Montgomery, 1938–
    The Christ of Christmas.

    Includes bibliographical references.
    1. Christmas sermons.   2. Presbyterian Church—
Sermons.   3. United Presbyterian Church in the U.S.A.—
Sermons.   4. Sermons, American.   I. Title.
BV4257.B62 1983   252′.61   83-13142
ISBN 0-8024-0337-9

P&R ISBN: 978-1-59638-159-9

To Immanuel

CONTENTS

Foreword   9

Preface   11

CHRIST AND CHRISTMAS

  1. The Christmas Story According to Jesus Christ   17

  2. What Child Is This?   27

THE VIRGIN BIRTH AND CHRISTMAS

  3. The Virgin Birth and History   39

  4. Matthew's Witness to the Virgin Birth   49

  5. The Genealogies   59

  6. The Virgin Birth and Christian Faith   69

THE FIRST CHRISTMAS

  7. The King in a Manger   81

  8. No Room in the Inn   93

  9. The Men Who Missed Christmas   103

 10. The Men Who Found Christmas   113

 11. The Gifts of Faith   125

 12. Returning Another Way   135

THE PEOPLE OF CHRISTMAS

13. Simeon's Psalm   147

14. The Little People of Christmas   157

15. How to Celebrate Christmas   167

16. The Indescribable Gift   179

$\mathcal{F}$OREWORD

MY HUSBAND Jim Boice loved Christmas. He loved everything about the Christmas season. For him celebrating Christmas was an expression of the joy every Christian should feel in remembering Jesus Christ's coming into the world to be our Savior. Jim knew that that was indeed something to celebrate.

He loved all the traditions of the Advent season. He would go caroling in our center-city neighborhood with members of Tenth Presbyterian Church, and enthusiastically supported the special programs presented by the children of the Sunday school. I cannot remember that he ever grumbled about commercialism; in fact, it was about the only time of the year when he shopped. No one was more the opposite of Dickens' character Scrooge than Jim was.

He threw himself into the yearly preparations, both at home and at Tenth. He and our three girls would choose our tree and then decorate it and the rest of the old manse and, later, our smaller house near the church in downtown Philadelphia. He loved the arrival of the towering spruce or fir in the sanctuary of Tenth that would fill one entire side of the platform, with no decorations except a small white or crimson bird placed high overhead on a branch.

For both of us, the high point of the season was the Christmas Eve service at Tenth Church. When we came there in 1968 there was no such service. A year or two after our arrival, however, an English friend came to Philadelphia to be Jim's secretary and was appalled that Tenth Church did not celebrate the birth of the Savior on December 24th or 25th. Jim gave this some thought and decided that Tenth should have a service, one early enough in the evening for families with young children. With the Session's approval that service was instituted, and it included candlelight, carefully chosen choir anthems, the reading of related Old and New Testament passages, and the full-throated singing of many beloved carols by the entire congregation. Over the years this service has grown, and now both members and non-members crowd the sanctuary.

But Jim especially cared about the Sunday services—that the hymns, special music, and messages would all help his congregation understand better and see afresh the glory of the Christmas story. He gave special effort to preparing clear, insightful sermons that would not be a rehash of old and tired material. The chapters in this volume have been developed from that hard work and prayerful preparation.

Jim's love of Christmas—which included, after hot chocolate and before the stockings were hung, reading with his family the wonderful birth account in Luke 2—was truly an expression of his joy and thankfulness for what God had done when He sent His son into the world to be Immanuel, the Savior of His people. The angels rejoiced at the time of Jesus' birth, and Jim felt that we, too, must rejoice and celebrate God's "indescribable gift."

Linda M. Boice
June 2009

PREFACE

OVER THE YEARS, it has been my privilege as a pastor preaching at the normal worship services of a local church to come repeatedly to the Christmas season and explore the Christmas story in a variety of ways. I confess that at times I have approached this task reluctantly, particularly in later years. I have wondered, having preached so many sermons on Luke 2, Matthew 2, and related "Christmas" passages, if I was going to be able to find anything new or even interesting for a congregation that has known those texts from childhood. But I have never been disappointed. I have always found the texts to speak in fresh ways first to me and then also, I hope, to the congregation.

The emphases I have found are not those normally associated with the Christmas accounts. Usually people think of Christmas in sentimental terms, focusing on the frailty of the baby or the beauties of motherhood. I have found the stories to be powerful and not at all sentimental.

The chief emphasis, as in all truly Christian theology, is on the deity of Christ—and the reason for which He came into the world on that first Christmas. Matthew identifies Jesus as "Immanuel . . . God with us" (Matthew 1:23). He shows how the wise men "worshiped" when they finally found Him (Matthew 2:11). Luke describes the mission of John the Baptist as preparing people "for the Lord" (Luke 1:17, 76). The angel who speaks to Mary calls Jesus "the Son of the Most High" (Luke 1:32), explaining how He is to be fathered by God's Holy Spirit (v. 35). Later, in the second chapter, the shepherds are pointed to one who is "a Savior," even "Christ the Lord" (v. 11). Simeon called Him God's salvation; "a light for revelation to the Gentiles and for glory to your people Israel" (Luke 2:32). If the babe of Christmas is God ("God with us"), then Christmas takes us back to Christ's pre-existence as the second Person of the Godhead, from all eternity, and forward to His work of salvation on the cross, His resurrection, and beyond. A theme like that is inexhaustible.

The second unique emphasis I have found in these stories is their concentration upon what I have called "the little people of Christmas." That is, there is very little weight given to the so-called important people of this world, like Caesar Augustus, Herod, the religious leaders of the day, or other leaders. Some of those come into the story indirectly, and others appear later in relationship to Christ and His ministry. But in this story the emphasis is upon "little people" like Joseph and Mary, the shepherds (who are not even named), Simeon, Anna, Zechariah, and Elizabeth. Even the wise men were not particularly important in terms of Jewish culture, for they were Gentiles, who were often assumed to have no part in Israel's spiritual blessings.

This second emphasis brings the Christmas story down to us, for most of us are not important in this world's eyes either. The story tells us that Jesus is for people like ourselves.

In putting this collection of Christmas messages in book form, I need to acknowledge that they have already been preached at Tenth Presbyterian Church—in Christmas seasons stretching from 1969 to 1982. Most have also appeared on the international radio program, "The Bible Study Hour," over roughly the same span of years. On occasion I have used one or a combination in addresses to various church and civic groups.

I know that the congregation of Tenth Presbyterian Church, which supports me in my many writing projects, joins me in praying that these studies might be a spiritual blessing to those who read them. I know they have been a blessing to me in my preparation. I wish to thank my secretary, Caecilie M. Foelster, for her effort and expertise in typing the manuscript and verifying the Scripture references.

"Thanks be to God for his indescribable gift!" (2 Corinthians 9:15).

CHRIST
AND
CHRISTMAS

I

THE CHRISTMAS STORY ACCORDING TO JESUS CHRIST

HAVE YOU EVER read the Christmas story according to Jesus Christ? I do not mean the Christmas story according to Luke, which we know so well, or Matthew, which we also know, or even the apostle John, but the Christmas story from the lips of the Lord Jesus Himself.

If we could meet the great personages of the Christmas story and interrogate them one by one, the story from each would be beautiful and stirring. Mary would have an account of the appearance of the angel, her trip to visit Elizabeth, the birth itself, the visit of the shepherds. Probably the early chapters of Luke give an account of those things as Mary herself told them. If we called the shepherds, they would be able to give us many details not in the biblical narrative, perhaps a description of the angels or the result of their later testimony to other people. Joseph would have his story. Yet having gone through all that interrogation, we would still want to hear from our Lord.

Where are we going to find that story? We do not have it in the gospels. The Lord's own story is in the Old Testament, in the fortieth psalm—and in the New Testament, which repeats these words in Hebrews:

Therefore, when Christ came into the world, he said:

"Sacrifice and offering you did not desire,
    but a body you prepared for me;
with burnt offerings and sin offerings
    you were not pleased.
Then I said, 'Here I am—it is written about me in the
        scroll—
    I have come to do your will, O God.'"
        (Hebrews 10:5–7)

That is what I call the Christmas story according to the Lord Jesus Christ.

BORN TO DIE

What is it that our Lord emphasizes in these verses? First, that He came into the world for a purpose. That is important, for it is uniquely true of Him. It cannot be said of any other person that he or she came into the world to do something. It is often true that there are purposes *parents* have for their children. They hope that the child lying in a crib will grow up to do something significant in this world. If the parents are Christians, they want their child to be kept from sin and be able to serve Jesus Christ. Parents have those and other aspirations. But the child does not have them. The child has to acquire them. That is why, from a Christian perspective, the child must be taught its destiny from the pages of the Word of God.

But Jesus was different. Our Lord says that He came (and was conscious of coming) for a specific purpose. Moreover, He spells that purpose out: "I have come *to do your will, O God.*"

What was that will? God willed Christ to be our Savior.

I do not know why it is, but we often lose a sense of that purpose in telling the Christmas story. We focus so much on the birth of the baby and on the sentiment that goes with that story—and there is a certain amount of legitimate sentimentality that goes with it—that we miss the most important things. Actually, the story is treated quite simply in Scripture, and the emphasis is always on the fact that Jesus came to die. The Lord Jesus Christ, the eternal Son of God, took a human body in order that He might die for our salvation. When our Lord speaks of His coming it is therefore highly understandable that He is thinking along those lines.

In the tenth chapter of Hebrews the author contrasts the sacrifices that took place in Israel before the coming of Christ—the sin offerings and burnt offerings, by which believers testified of their faith that God would accept them on the basis of the death of an innocent substitute—with Christ's great and perfect sacrifice. It is in the context of that contrast, between the former things and that which has now come, between the shadow and the reality, that he brings in the quotation from Psalm 40. The Lord Jesus Christ came into this world with a purpose, and that purpose was to do God's will: to be our Savior. We miss the most important thing about Christmas if we fail to see that.

WHO CAN PAY?

A second point emerges from these verses. It is not only that our Lord came into the world with a sense of purpose; He also came into the world with knowledge that He was the perfect one to fulfill that purpose.

It is possible to have a noble purpose and yet not be the one to fulfill it. We see that many times when we talk to children. They are aware of what they want to do, but often they cannot quite do it. They will say, "Here, let me do it! I can do it!" But they cannot do it, and after they have struggled a bit—wise parents let them struggle—they must be helped to fulfill the task. That was not the case with Jesus Christ. As He came into the world, our Lord had His mind on His great purpose: to provide salvation for the race. But not only did He have the purpose in mind, He also was aware that He was the one perfectly suited to carry out that purpose. He was perfectly suited by virtue of who He was. Unlike anybody else who has ever been born, He was not only man; He was God as well. Therefore while as a man He could die upon the cross, as God He died in order to pay the infinite price necessary for our salvation.

Harry Ironside used to tell about a young man who was a soldier in the Russian army. Because the young man's father was a friend of Czar Nicholas I, the young man had been given a rather responsible post. He was paymaster in one of the barracks for the Russian army, and it was his responsibility to see that the right amount of money was distributed each month to the soldiers. The young man meant well, but his character was not up to his responsibility. He took to gambling. Eventually he had gambled away a great deal of the government's money as well as all his own.

In due course the young man received notice that a representative of the czar was coming to check the accounts, and he knew that he was in trouble. That evening he got out the books and totaled up the funds owed. Then he went to the safe and got out his own pitifully small amount of money. As he sat there and looked at the two he was overwhelmed at the astronomical debt versus his own small change. He was ruined! He knew he would be disgraced. At last the young man determined to take his life. He pulled out his revolver, placed it on the table before him, and wrote a summation of his misdeeds. At the bottom of the ledger, where he had totaled up his illegal borrowings, he wrote: "A great debt! Who can pay?" He decided that at the stroke of midnight he would die.

As the evening wore on the young soldier grew drowsy and eventually fell asleep. That night Czar Nicholas I, as was sometimes his custom, was making the rounds of this particular barracks. Seeing a light, he stopped, looked in, and saw the young man asleep. He recognized him immediately and, looking over his shoulder, saw the ledger book and realized all that had taken place. He was about to awaken him and put him under arrest when his eye fastened on the young man's message: "A great debt! Who can pay?" Suddenly, with a surge of magnanimity he reached over, wrote one word at the bottom of the ledger, and slipped out.

The young man was sleeping fitfully. He awoke suddenly in the middle of the night, glanced at the clock and, realizing that it was long after midnight, reached for his revolver to shoot himself. But as he did so his eye fell upon the ledger. He saw something that he had not seen before. There was his writing: "A great debt! Who can pay?" But underneath it was the word the czar had written: "Nicholas."

He was dumbfounded. He did not understand how it could have got there. There must be some mistake. He went to the safe where material that bore the signature of the czar was on file. It was the czar's signature. He said to himself, "The czar must have come by when I was asleep. He has seen the book. He knows all. Still he is willing to forgive me." The young soldier then rested on the word of the czar, and the next morning a messenger came from the palace with exactly the amount needed to meet the deficit. Only the czar could pay, and the czar did pay.[1]

In the same way only the Lord Jesus Christ was able to pay our debt to God. We look at the moral requirement of God's righteousness spelled out in His law. We compare it with our own tawdry performance, and we ask the question: "A great debt to God! Who can pay?" But then the Lord Jesus

1. H. A. Ironside, *Illustrations of Bible Truth* (Chicago: Moody, 1945), pp. 67–69.

Christ steps forward and signs His name to our ledger: "Jesus Christ." Only Jesus can pay, and He does.

Joy Unspeakable

The third thing in this text is that Jesus was delighted to do the Father's will. That very word is in some of our versions. It is certainly in the fortieth psalm. We find in many places in Scripture that the Lord was *satisfied* in His ministry. The twenty-second psalm describes His death by crucifixion, and toward the end of that psalm He is praising God. The fifty-third chapter of Isaiah perhaps better than any other Old Testament passage spells out the theme of vicarious atonement, the death of one on behalf of the many. At the end of that chapter we find Jesus looking upon the travail of His soul and saying, "I am 'satisfied'" (Isaiah 53:11). Hebrews 10:5–7 tells us He actually *delighted* to do the will of God.

Could Jesus be delighted to come to this earth from glory, to lay aside all the privileges and prerogatives He had enjoyed as the eternal Son of God, to take to Himself a human form, to become like us, to become poor, to suffer throughout life, and then eventually to suffer upon the cross and die the death of a sinner, a malefactor, an evildoer? Yes, Jesus delighted in that, because it was His pleasure to do the Father's will to achieve our salvation.

Imagine a person who sees something to be done and recognizes that he or she is the one to do it, but then either does not do it or does it reluctantly. The person says, "Well,

I suppose it has to be done, and I guess I'm the only one able to do it. Nobody else will do it if I don't. So, all right, I'll do it." The work is done, but there was no joy in it. I am glad our Lord did not think like that. Our Lord did not say, "Well, Father, I suppose that if this is what You want and if You haven't got anybody else, I'll go die." It was not like that at all. Jesus delighted to do the Father's will. It was His joy to bring the sons and daughters of God into glory.

Is it any wonder that the angels were joyful as they announced the coming of that one who was to be the Savior?

We too should be joyful, not because we give gifts to one another, not because there is a certain lightheartedness or Christmas spirit in the world at large, not because there is a pretty story that is nice to tell children, but because Jesus Christ was joyful as He came into the world to be our Savior. If He was joyful, we should be joyful as well.

"I AM WITH YOU ALWAYS"

There is one more thing to notice. When the Lord says, "Here I am," He is speaking in the present tense, which is undoubtedly intended to make this important point: "I have come; but not only have I come, I have come never to depart again."

Edmund P. Clowney, the former president of Westminster Theological Seminary, had been speaking about Christ to some individual. The person said, "The problem I have with Christianity is that it all happened so long ago. You're talking about something that happened two thousand years ago. If Christ had only been born, say, a hundred years ago, it would be different." Dr. Clowney's response was the correct one. He said, "Those events that happened so long ago have not ceased to be current. Rather, the Lord Jesus Christ, who came then, comes again and again through the person of His Holy Spirit to bring the accomplishment of His salvation to the individual."

That is the reason the Christmas story is alive. It is the only reason it has the hold it has upon so many millions of people.

If the story were a fable or even an event that merely had happened 2,000 years ago (or even 100 years ago) and then ended, it would have no hold upon us. What does it really matter that somebody died long ago in a far-off land? I have my problems. You have your problems. So what? But if the One who came then still comes, if He comes to the individual through His Spirit to bring the results of the salvation He accomplished 2,000 years ago to where you and I stand and act now, then this story lives and enables us to live also.

Have you found the Lord Jesus Christ, who came at Christmas, to be your Savior? Have you placed your trust in Him? He has come. He can be yours in this moment. Phillips Brooks, in his carol "O Little Town of Bethlehem," has a stanza that is a delight at this point.

How silently, how silently
    The wondrous gift is giv'n!
So God imparts to human hearts
    The blessings of His heav'n.

No ear may hear His coming.
    But in this world of sin,
Where meek souls will receive Him still,
    The dear Christ enters in.

So He does! May this be your experience at this Christmas season.

2

WHAT CHILD IS THIS?

THE FIRST CHAPTER of Matthew begins with a genealogy of the Lord Jesus Christ followed immediately by an account of His birth. With the exception of that genealogy, the first words of the entire New Testament are these: "This is how the birth of Jesus Christ came about. His mother Mary was pledged to be married to Joseph, but before they came together, she was found to be with child through the Holy Spirit" (Matthew 1:18).

What a remarkable beginning to the account of Jesus' life! There is no doubt that Jesus was a man. The listing of His genealogy is itself ample proof of that; He was descended from Abraham through Abraham's great descendant King David. Jesus was as human as we are.

Yet if those words are true, as we obviously are to believe they are, then something more needs to be said. Matthew is speaking of a man, but of a man born without benefit of a human father. The male part in the conception of Jesus was taken over by the Holy Spirit of God. No one in the whole history of the human race was conceived that way. Yet here is Matthew speaking of one who was as distinguished from us by the beginning of His earthly life as we know He also was by the end.

Who is Jesus Christ?

What child is this, who, laid to rest,
    On Mary's lap is sleeping?
Whom angels greet with anthems sweet,
    While shepherds watch are keeping?

Where are we to go for an answer? Should we ask the theologians? They will not help us much, for they disagree on their answers, as we know. Some have a divine Jesus, some a merely human one. Some speak of "*the myth* of God incarnate." Once I heard J. I. Packer of Regent College, Vancouver, British Columbia, pray, "O Lord, deliver us from theological notions." I said "amen" to that, for notions are precisely what many theological opinions are. They are like the "notions" counter in a department store—random collections of more or less whimsical objects—and not nearly as lasting.

Shall we go to the Pharisees or scribes of the Christmas story? Shall we ask Herod? Those are mere men, no better (and perhaps less) informed than our contemporary theologians. Let us be done with these lesser personages and turn to those who ought to know and who, in fact, appear in the Christmas story for the express purpose of answering our question.

THE ANGEL GABRIEL

Gabriel, the angel of God, appears at least twice in the Christmas story, once to announce the birth of John the Baptist to John's father, the aged Zechariah, and once to announce the birth of Jesus to Mary. It is the second annunciation that bears on our question, for, having appeared to Mary and having greeted her as one "highly favored" of the Lord, the angel went on to say, "Do not be afraid, Mary, you have found favor with God. You will be with child and give birth to a son, and you are to give him the name Jesus. He will be great and will be called the Son of the Most High. The Lord God will give him the throne of his father David, and he will reign over the house of Jacob forever; his kingdom will never end" (Luke 1:30–33).

Each of those pronouncements must have struck the young virgin as remarkable. It was remarkable that her son would be great, she being of humble origins. It was remarkable that He would reign on the throne of David forever. Everyone knew that God had promised David that he would have an heir to reign on his throne forever; but that had not yet happened. In Mary's day the house of David had been cast down, and foreigners ruled the land. If Gabriel was right in telling Mary that her son would reign on David's throne, the long waiting of the Jewish people was now over and their Messiah had come. Mary's future child was that Messiah. All that was remarkable. But those were not the most remarkable parts of Gabriel's greeting. The most astonishing thing was that the child was to be "the Son of the Most High."

Were it not for the context, a person might be inclined to take this in a minimal sense, that is, as speaking of one merely chosen by God to fulfill a special task. It was used of Israel in just that way (Psalm 82:6; Jeremiah 31:20). It was used of the kings (2 Samuel 7:14). In this case, however, the context has to do with the conception of Mary's child without a human father. His Father would be God Himself, for He would be "the Son of the Most High." In other words, the child was to be God's offspring in a way no other person either before or since has been.

If we had only the context of Gabriel's annunciation to Mary, the promise would be remarkable enough. But that is not our only context. We also have the whole of the New Testament in which this title is picked up and explained.

We think of Peter's confession of Christ. Jesus had asked the disciples who they thought He was, and Peter replied, "You are the Christ, the Son of the living God" (Matthew 16:16). This was no mere earthly sonship, for Jesus indicated that Peter's insight was so remarkable that it had come not from Peter's own powers of observation, but by revelation from God: "Blessed are you, Simon son of Jonah, for this was not revealed to you by man, but by my Father in heaven" (v. 17). By the illumination of God, Peter had perceived that Jesus was no mere man but very God. He was God incarnate.

We find the fullest New Testament treatment in 1 John. The Christians to whom John wrote had been shaken by teachers who claimed to be believers who were denying that Jesus was "God . . . come in the flesh" (1 John 4:2–3). They were troubled by those denials, and John wrote to them to assure them that they, rather than the false teachers, were actually God's children. The false teachers are of Antichrist, who always denies Christ's divinity, John says. Christians can know they are of God by their conviction that Jesus is indeed God's Son. John puts it in formula form: "If anyone acknowledges that Jesus is the Son of God, God lives in him and he in God. And so we know and rely on the love God has for us" (1 John 4:15–16). "Jesus is the Son of God" becomes the confession by which one can tell whether or not one is actually a Christian.

When Gabriel told Mary that the future child would be "the Son of the Most High," he was saying that the child would be God.

Joseph's Angel

The angel who appeared to Joseph is described in Matthew 1:18–24. This angel may have been Gabriel, but he is not named. He is only "an angel" who appears to say, "Joseph son of David, do not be afraid to take Mary home as your wife, because what is conceived in her is from the Holy Spirit. She will give birth to a son, and you are to give him the name Jesus, because he will save his people from their sins" (Matthew 1:20–21).

This revelation is similar to the revelation to Mary, for the title *Jesus*, just as *Son of God*, has a general and human as well as a specific and divine application. *Jesus* means "Jehovah is salvation," or "Jehovah saves." It is a testimony to the truth that salvation is of the Lord (cf. Jonah 2:9). This appellation was used by many people. *Joshua* is a variant of the same name, for example. But that cannot be the full meaning of the name in Matthew 1:21, for here the angel is explaining the virgin conception of Christ. That is, the name is in part an explanation of what is happening. It is a case of God at work. Moreover, immediately after giving the child the name *Jesus*, meaning "Jehovah saves," the angel goes on to say in reference to the child, "He will save his people from their sins." In other words, "He [the child] is Jehovah."

This revelation to Joseph is confirmed by Matthew as he continues the narration, for he says that it happened to fulfill what God had prophesied through Isaiah: "The virgin will be with child and will give birth to a son, and will call him Immanuel" (Isaiah 7:14), which means, as Matthew points out, "God with us" (Matthew 1:23).

THE SHEPHERDS' ANGEL

If anyone should know who Mary's child is, it is certainly the angels, God's messengers. An angel appeared to the shepherds as they were watching their sheep in the fields surrounding Bethlehem. This angel said, "Do not be afraid. I bring you good news of great joy that will be for all the people. Today in the town of David a Savior has been born to you; he is Christ the Lord" (Luke 2:10–11).

This is one of the most significant texts in the New Testament, for through a small grammatical detail (directed by the Holy Spirit, who inspired the biblical writers) two words give the fullest possible testimony to Jesus' divinity. When the angel said to the shepherds that the child who had been born in Bethlehem was "Christ the Lord," the Greek words read *Christos kyrios*. The ending of both words is masculine and in the nominative case, thus making the words equivalents. If instead of this we had read *Christos kyriou*, which is a very common way of writing—that is, with the first word in the nominative case and the second in the genitive—the phrase would mean "the Lord's Christ." This would be an appropriate way to refer to anyone anointed to a special task in Israel as God's prophet, priest, or king. David would be "the Lord's Christ," for example. But that is not what the phrase says. Instead of reading "the Lord's Christ," we actually read, "Christ the Lord," which means "Christ, *who is* the Lord."

The sentence means that He, who by this time had already been born of Mary, was not merely the anointed one of God but was actually God now manifest in human form.

Gabriel appeared to Mary and announced that the child was to be *God's Son*. The angel who appeared to Joseph said that He would be *Jehovah who saves*. The angel who told the shepherds of Christ's birth called Him *the Lord*. Three angels! Three testimonies! And the testimonies agree that Jesus is God.

GOD THE FATHER

There is one more person we want to ask about this matter, and that is the Father Himself. We can imagine a case in which the parentage of a child is disputed and the question is therefore finally put to the alleged father, "Are you the father of this child?" Jesus has been declared to be the unique child of God by three appearances of an angel. We are inclined to believe angels, though in such a case we might find the word of mere human beings questionable. But what of the Father? What does He say? Does He acknowledge Jesus of Nazareth as His Son?

That direct word is not given in the Christmas story, though everything in it may be said rightly to have come to us from God. Instead we have to wait for thirty years, until the Lord began His ministry.

After the events of those early years, which included the murder of the innocents and the flight into Egypt, Jesus was brought back to Nazareth, where He lived in Joseph's home and presumably learned Joseph's trade. He grew to manhood "in wisdom and stature, and in favor with God and men" (Luke 2:52). One day He appeared at the Jordan River, where His cousin John had been preaching and baptizing. He presented Himself for baptism, which John was reluctant to do. John said, "I need to be baptized by you, and do you come to me?" (Matthew 3:14). Jesus said that it was proper for him to do this since He had come to "fulfill all righteousness."

So John baptized Jesus. As Jesus came up out of the water, at that moment heaven was opened, the Spirit of God descended like a dove upon Him, and a voice from heaven was heard saying, "This is my Son, whom I love; with him I am well pleased" (v. 17). *This is My Son!* It was the voice of God, God's testimony. The angels had announced this truth; now the Father Himself confirmed it. In the mouth of two or three witnesses, and those of the greatest and most trustworthy character, Jesus' sonship was established.

OUR TESTIMONY

Only one thing remains: not to seek for further witnesses, but meekly to add our confession to God's own. Is this child of Christmas God's Son? Is He God with us? Then let us acknowledge Him as such. Let us worship Him and show by the obedience of our lives that He is indeed who He is declared so clearly to be.

Thomas did it. There was a time when Thomas was not certain of his confession. Early in Christ's ministry, when He had chosen His disciples and had set about to preach the ways of God's kingdom, Thomas had believed in Jesus. He would have echoed Peter's confession: "You are the Christ, the Son of the living God" (Matthew 16:16). But things did not go as Thomas had expected, and the day came when Jesus was crucified, an outcome totally unexpected by Thomas. His world was shattered. Therefore, three days later when someone said that Jesus had been raised from the dead, Thomas would not believe it. At this point in his life Thomas would have given his creed in four words, "Dead men don't rise." But Jesus had risen, whether Thomas believed it or not, and the day came when Jesus appeared to Thomas himself. Jesus presented Himself for examination, and Thomas, who a moment before had been an utter skeptic, fell down before Him, confessing, "My Lord and My God!" (John 20:28).

That is what you and I must do. We must confess Jesus to be God, and more than that—to be *our* God, and our *Lord* besides. We must say with the centurion present at the crucifixion, "Surely he was the Son of God!" (Matthew 27:54). Like Paul we must acknowledge Him as Lord (Acts 9:5)! We must confess Him as Thomas did, when he exclaimed: "My Lord and my God!"

> What child is this, who, laid to rest,
>   on Mary's lap is sleeping?
> Whom angels greet with anthems sweet,
>   while shepherds watch are keeping?

The hymn writer knew, for the verse goes on:

> This, this is Christ the King,
>   Whom shepherds guard and angels sing:
> This, this is Christ the King,
>   The babe, the Son of Mary.

> So bring Him incense, gold and myrrh,
>   Come, peasant, king, to own Him;
> The King of kings salvation brings,
>   Let loving hearts enthrone Him.

> This, this is Christ the King,
>   Whom shepherds guard and angels sing:
> This, this is Christ the King,
>   The babe, the Son of Mary.

THE VIRGIN BIRTH AND CHRISTMAS

3

THE VIRGIN BIRTH AND HISTORY

Silent night! holy night!
All is calm, all is bright
'Round yon virgin mother and Child.

—JOSEPH MOHR

THUS DO WE SING each Christmas! And thus also do we profess belief in the virgin birth of Jesus as part of the Christmas story. But is it a true part of Christmas? Is it even true? And if it is, what is its proper place in the whole spectrum of Christian theology?

In the early decades of the twentieth century the virgin birth was the focal point of many of the denials of Christian truth by liberalism. Those who believed the Word of God and recognized that the virgin birth is in the Word rose to its defense in those decades and did a very good job. It was so well defended, in fact, that in recent times liberals have refused even to grapple with the arguments raised on behalf of this great truth of the faith. Things have gone on without much thought about it, but that is in spite of the fact that belief in the virgin birth was part and parcel of Christianity in earlier centuries and that the Scriptures speak so clearly about it.

The earliest intimation of the virgin birth is in Genesis 3:15, in that first announcement of the deliverer who would come. It was said that He would be the offspring of "the woman." Admittedly, this text does not explicitly teach the virgin birth. It does not explicitly exclude a male parent. But it is significant that a male parent is not mentioned and that the one to come is called merely the woman's offspring.

In Isaiah 7:14 a prophecy spoken to Ahaz says that a virgin would conceive and bear a son and that his name would be called Immanuel, which is "God with us." Some scholars have criticized interpretations that relate this text to the virgin birth on the grounds that that Hebrew word translated "virgin" is 'almah, which can also mean a young woman of marriageable age, though not necessarily a virgin. (There is another Hebrew word that would be more explicit, but it may be that the choice of words was deliberate for the sake of Ahaz. There may have been a person who did give birth to a son who was not in any way miraculously overshadowed by the Holy Spirit.)

But when we come to the New Testament we find that text cited by Matthew as referring to the virgin birth of Jesus. Thus he endorses the virgin birth interpretation. Matthew used a Greek term that can *only* mean "virgin," one who has never had intercourse with a man.

Several Old Testament texts lead up to the New Testament doctrine, and then in the early chapters of Luke and Matthew the doctrine of the virgin birth is fully unfolded.

Belief and Unbelief

The doctrine of the virgin birth is not neglected today because it has been disproved. Quite the opposite is the case. It is disregarded out of simple unbelief. When the battle was being waged between the growing forces of liberalism and the conservatives, or fundamentalists, J. Gresham Machen wrote a definitive book on the subject called *The Virgin Birth of Christ*.[1] In that book, with that scholarly precision for which he was known and in a way analogous only to the careful scholarship of a man like John Owen or B. B. Warfield, Machen established the historical foundations for this teaching and destroyed any argument that could possibly be raised on the other side. His book has two parts: first, a historical part in which data is derived from the birth narratives in Luke and Matthew, and then a second, polemical part in which Machen refutes suggestions that belief in the virgin birth could have entered Christianity from pagan mythology or Judaism.

Machen did his work so well that years later, at Harvard University, one of the professors in the School of Divinity

1. J. Gresham Machen, *The Virgin Birth of Christ* (1930; reprint, London; James Clarke, 1958).

pointed out (even though he did not endorse Machen's conclusions) that nobody had ever answered Machen's arguments.

When people do not want to believe something they often simply do not answer the arguments. They say, "We've progressed beyond that," or, "We've come to see things differently today." That is dishonest. No one has the right to say, "We have gone beyond that," until he has answered the arguments the man before has raised. If we fail to do that, our new beliefs are mere arrogance. We can advance in knowledge, but we do not advance until we first come to terms with what has gone before.

A HEBREW SOURCE

If the virgin birth is historical, the place to begin is with the documents. So we start with Luke's testimony. What can be said about the early chapters of this gospel?

Luke was a Greek. Moreover, he was apparently a very careful historian. In Acts, where we are able to check his history by its correlation with other material from the time, we find that Luke is extraordinarily accurate. Conservatives would say that Luke is an inerrant historian. But even from the point of view of those who do not believe in inerrancy, Luke is reliable.

We learn from Acts also that Luke was Paul's companion. In certain passages Luke, having written of the travels of Paul in the third person, saying, "*He* went here," or, "*He* did that," switched over to the first person and began to use the word *we* instead, saying, "*We* did this," or, "*We* did that." The first example is in Acts 16:10. Most people understand that Luke was indicating that at those particular points he joined Paul in his travels. If that is correct, we know Luke accompanied Paul to Jerusalem (Acts 21) and therefore, like Paul, also met James and had conversation with others who had known the Lord personally. James was the Lord's brother.

Luke had a historical interest, wrote accurately, and had opportunity to talk with those who knew Jesus Christ in the flesh. Undoubtedly he would have made inquiries to find out what happened in the early days of our Lord's life and even before His birth.

When we come to the early chapters of Luke we find such stories. But it is interesting how we find them. The first four verses of Luke are written in what has often been described as a perfect Greek sentence.

Greek is a beautiful language and is somewhat like German in that it uses numerous participles to introduce and link up dependent clauses. Like German, it is possible for Greek to go on verse after verse without any periods and finally end with a thunderous crescendo, emphasizing the point of the passage. That is what Luke does in these opening verses. Some of our translations disguise this by breaking up the sentence. The *New International Version* has two sentences. But in the Greek it is all one.

We get a better idea of what the Greek sounds like from the King James Version, for it usually adheres to the Greek word order. It says, "Forasmuch as many have taken in hand to set forth in order a declaration of those things which are most surely believed among us, even as they delivered them unto us, which from the beginning were eyewitnesses, and ministers of the word; it seemed good to me also, having had perfect understanding of all things from the very first, to write unto thee in order, most excellent Theophilus, that thou mightest know the certainty of those things, wherein thou has been instructed" (Luke 1:1–4, KJV).

The interesting thing, however, is that after that introduction, verse 5 immediately introduces something entirely different, something utterly unanticipated. Beginning with verse 5 and continuing through the end of chapter 2, that is, throughout the important opening section of Luke's gospel, we find, not the Greek style of writing that has been found in the first four verses, the very thing we would anticipate of Luke, but rather a style that is obviously Jewish or Semitic.

Machen says, "The prologue of the gospel, embracing the first four verses, is one of the most carefully constructed sentences in the whole New Testament. . . . It would be difficult to imagine a more skillfully formed, and more typically Greek sentence than this. Yet this typically Greek sentence is followed by what is probably the most markedly Semitic section in the whole New Testament."[2]

Semitic literary style has a number of interesting characteristics. One is called *parataxis*, "laying something alongside something else." That is, one sentence usually follows another without interwoven subordinate clauses. As we reach such sentences the most noticeable feature is the frequent use of the word *and*, such as in Luke 1:5–2:52. Again in the *New International Version* that is not so evident because the translators have tried to break up things a bit. But we do find it in the King James Version. Here is a sample, beginning with Luke 1:5: "There was in the days of Herod, the king of Judaea, a certain priest named Zacharias, of the course of Abia [Abijah]; *and* his wife

2. Ibid., p. 46.

was of the daughters of Aaron, *and* her name was Elisabeth. *And* they were both righteous before God, walking in all the commandments and ordinances of the Lord blameless. *And* they had no child, because that Elisabeth was barren, *and* they both were now well stricken in years" (emphasis added). There is an obvious change in style.

There is another difference in the style here. It is what is called *parallelism*. That is very common in Hebrew writing, especially poetry. A sentence is given, then a second sentence that says virtually the same thing but in slightly different words. We see that in Mary's Magnificat (1:46–55), for example. "My soul praises the Lord and my spirit rejoices in God my Savior" (v. 46). In that sentence virtually the same thing is said twice in parallel construction. Again, in verse 51: "He has performed mighty deeds with his arm; he has scattered those who are proud in their inmost thoughts." Verses 52–53: "He has brought down rulers from their thrones but has lifted up the humble. He has filled the hungry with good things but has sent the rich away empty."

If we understand style and carefully read these chapters we recognize that Luke has somehow incorporated into his usual Greek-style narrative something that is obviously not Greek but that derives from some other source.

Moreover, not only the style but also the subject matter indicates a change. In reading these chapters, one of the first things we notice is that they are moving not in a Christian environment, the kind of thing that we would expect of a writer who was describing these events long after they had happened and in view of Christ's later ministry, but in a pre-Christian environment.

For example, there is the barrenness of Elizabeth introduced at the beginning and explained later in relation to God's favor or lack of it. Elizabeth says, "In these days he [God] has shown his favor and taken away my disgrace among the people" (v. 25). That is a Jewish idea. To be a married woman and to be barren was a disgraceful thing. But that was not the case among the Greeks.

Again, there is the announcement of the angel to Zechariah (1:13–17). This is pre-Christian, because the angel speaks of the future in terms of the expectations of Jews within the covenant nation of Israel. We find the same thing in the Magnificat. In those verses we find not a single specific intimation of what the Lord Jesus Christ was to do. They do not mention His ministry. They do not mention His death or resurrection. Instead there is praise to God in language that would have been common to Mary and the Jews of her day, but would not have been common in the later Christian church. A final example is Simeon's prayer in the Temple after Jesus is born. He calls this child "a light for revelation to the Gentiles and for glory to your people Israel" (Luke 2:32). This too is Jewish. Nothing in this verse betrays the full expansion of the gospel to the Gentiles that by the time of Luke had taken place as the result of Christianity.

WHAT IS THEIR ORIGIN?

That leads to the question, If these things are here and if they do not fit stylistically into what we would normally expect from Luke, who writes good Greek prose, where did Luke acquire these particular facts and perhaps even these particular documents?

We have to go back to the fact that Luke was undoubtedly a keen historian. He was used to making careful investigations. He says as much in the prologue, for he writes: "I myself have carefully investigated everything from the beginning" (Luke 1:3). He was not merely reporting stories or rumors but was relating facts he had carefully investigated and searched out. How did Luke do it? Where did he get these particular facts? He undoubtedly got them from talking with those who were eyewitnesses of the earthly ministry of Jesus Christ. In the case of the narratives of Christ's birth, Luke presumably got them from Mary, who would be the original and best of all eyewitnesses. Moreover, he presumably got them in some kind of written version, which may also go back to Mary in some way.

THE UNIQUE CHRIST

A number of conclusions follow. First, the idea of the virgin birth is not some later addition to Christianity but is present in the earliest sources. People often try to undermine Christianity by saying of important doctrines, "This is only something that has been tacked on later by people who found it to be a pious way of representing some subjective experience."

Rudolf Bultmann is one who goes to the extreme in this particular approach, because in Bultmann's theology everything in the New Testament falls into this category. Bultmann will not acknowledge that anything in the New Testament has any relationship to the historical Jesus. He speaks only of the mere "thatness" of Christ's existence. He acknowledges that there was a Christ, but that is all he will say about Him. What we have in the New Testament is different. It is the expression in historical narration of what really happened.

Second, the virgin birth was not invented by Luke (or any other early writer) but was learned by him from the earliest and most reliable of all witnesses—presumably Mary herself, or at least those to whom she passed on the information.

If that is true, we conclude that the virgin birth is a fact of history. We recognize, of course, that people do not like facts that fail to correspond with their own experience. If they fail to conform, these facts are presumed to have no basis, and skeptics are ready to dispense with them as myth. But that is not a wise procedure. Shakespeare's Hamlet said, "There are more things in heaven and earth . . . than are dreamt of in your philosophy" (act 1 sc. 5, line 167). People often have a limited philosophy. Many things do not enter into it. But that does not mean that they are untrue. So when we are dealing with these great doctrines of Christianity we must recognize that, in spite of contemporary unbelief, the virgin birth has a place in history.

Fourth, the virgin birth is important because of its unique and miraculous nature, which therefore points to the uniqueness of Jesus Christ. It is significant that the life of the Lord Jesus is bracketed by two great miracles. At the beginning is the virgin birth: He comes into being without benefit of a human father, and so is the Son of God and son of man in a unique way. At the end is the resurrection: He conquers and transcends the greatest of all enemies, death. What clearer way did God have of drawing attention to this one who is unique in human history?

Matthew's Witness to the Virgin Birth

As we begin to study Matthew's account of the birth of Christ we must remind ourselves of what has already been learned from Luke's narrative. We saw as we studied Luke 1 and 2 that those chapters are unique in having a strongly Semitic style and theology so that they can rightly be called pre-Christian. Where did Luke obtain this material?

Luke was not a disciple of the Lord. He was a Greek. He came to Christianity through the ministry of the apostle Paul and traveled with Paul, probably having his first exposure to Palestine when he traveled there with Paul somewhat late in Paul's missionary travels. The logical place to assume that Luke got his information about the virgin birth—though he fails to say so himself—is through conversation with those who in their own experience reached back to the beginning of the Lord's life and ministry. These chapters probably bear the flavor of Mary's own experience and testimony.

Luke's material says certain interesting things about the virgin birth. It tells us that it is not a later addition to Christianity (because it is found in the earliest sources), and it tells us that it is a fact of history that, being unique and miraculous, points quite naturally to the unique nature of our Lord Jesus Christ. The virgin birth tells us that Jesus is the unique Son of God.

MATTHEW'S NARRATIVE

From this background we turn to Matthew, where the second of the two New Testament accounts of the virgin birth is found. This is equally clear in terms of its central teaching. But when we compare it with Luke's account we find a number of interesting dissimilarities as well as similarities.

The first thing we discover as we begin to look at these verses is that they, no less than Luke 1:5–2:52, are Jewish in character. For example, the very first mention of the birth of Christ (following the genealogy that begins chapter 1) introduces the betrothal of Joseph and Mary and explains the peculiar difficulty in which Joseph found himself when he realized that Mary was expecting a child and that he was not the father. He naturally suspected sin on her part and was determined to divorce her privately. That is very Jewish, because it points to a circumstance in Jewish culture that did not prevail in the Greek or Roman world. Joseph and Mary were not married; yet the betrothal carried such weight of personal commitment on their parts as well as on the parts of their families that in order to dissolve the engagement there had to be something almost like a divorce. The very first verses of Matthew's account of the birth are inexplicable apart from this concept.

As we read on, we notice that five times in these opening two chapters Matthew explains what is happening by reference to the Old Testament. He says, "This took place to fulfill what the Lord had said through the prophet . . ." (1:22; cf. 2:5, 15, 17, 23), and then quotes an Old Testament passage that prophesied what he had just narrated. Matthew 1:22 introduces a quotation from Isaiah 7:14—"The virgin will be with child and will give birth to a son, and they will call him Immanuel" (v. 23). Matthew 2:5 introduces a quotation from Micah 5:2—"But you, Bethlehem, in the land of Judah, are by no means least among the rulers of Judah; for out of you will come a ruler who will be the shepherd of my people Israel" (v. 6). We find the same thing in verse 15, where there is a reference to Hosea 11:1; in verse 18, where there is a reference to Jeremiah 31:15; and in verse 23, where there is a reference to the prophecy that Jesus would be called a Nazarene (the Old Testament text is uncertain). Each of these quotations indicates the book's essentially Jewish character.

But there is a difference between these chapters and the corresponding chapters in Luke. In Luke's gospel, the Semitic, Jewish chapters are clearly out of place. In Matthew's gospel, they are not at all out of place, for the gospel from beginning to end is Jewish. We have similarity in style but great differences in regard to authorship.

There is another distinction, too. When we were looking at the first and second chapters of Luke we saw that their content and atmosphere are pre-Christian. Missing are all characteristics of postresurrection Christianity. Everything is Jewish. On the other hand, when we turn to Matthew's gospel, though it is also strictly Jewish in style, it is clear that it is post-Christian, because from the very beginning there is a clear anticipation that the one to be born would die for sin. His name would be "Jesus, because he will save his people from their sins" (Matthew 1:21).

The story of the wise men, found in Matthew and in no other gospel, reflects the same outlook. The significance of the magi's coming is that they were Gentiles. So Matthew at the very beginning indicates that the gospel is for everyone.

TRUE OR FALSE ACCOUNTS

What is the relationship between those two accounts? Whenever I consider parallel accounts (like these or others in the Bible), I think of the way Reuben A. Torrey used to handle parallel accounts when he was speaking about the resurrection. He pointed out that parallel accounts must have been produced by one of three methods: either they are invented, in which case they were either invented in collusion (the people getting together to write their accounts) or separately (that is, independently of each other); or they were not invented at all but are records of observed events.[1]

1. Reuben A. Torrey, *The Bible and Its Christ* (New York; Revell, 1904), pp. 58–85. See also J. Gresham Machen, *The Virgin Birth of Christ* (1930; reprint, London: James Clarke, 1958), pp. 188–209.

Let us ask into which of those three categories Luke's and Matthew's accounts of the virgin birth fit.

Let us assume that these are *invented accounts*, mythology. Liberal scholars would say that sometime late in the history of Christian thought, perhaps after the first generation of Christians had gone by, men and women had begun to reflect on the significance of Jesus' coming. They may have said, "We have to have some way of indicating that His life was extraordinary; let's invent a virgin birth as a symbolic expression of the uniqueness of the Christ event." Let us assume that the accounts were invented and ask whether they were invented in collusion or separately.

There are different ways of doing things in collusion. Matthew and Luke could have met in Jerusalem. Luke could have said to Matthew, "You know, Matthew, I'm writing a gospel about Jesus Christ. I want to tell His story, and I'm writing something about His origins, something about His birth." Matthew could have replied, "That's very interesting, Luke, because I'm doing the same thing. I'm writing something about Christ and about His birth, and, you know, there's not much information around anymore. I thought that I would make up a story that would indicate how these things might go." Luke would then say to Matthew, "Since we're in the same situation, let's get together and work these stories out. We don't want to write two contrary accounts. Let's make sure we say the same thing. Because if you say one thing and I say another, who's going to believe us?" That is one way in which collusion could come about.

There is another way in which it could happen. We could suppose that Matthew wrote his account and then died. Luke then came to Jerusalem and, while rummaging around among papers, found Matthew's gospel. He said, "Here's some source material. I'll make up an account that uses this material." That is a second kind of collusion.

Third, there is a historical, literary kind of collusion in which we can suppose that Matthew and Luke never met and did not use each other's books, but somehow both got hold of a document that was floating around Jerusalem.

If Matthew and Luke made those accounts up, would there be the kind of noticeable, apparent, discrepancies we find? Luke talks about an annunciation: an angel appearing to Mary to explain that a child was going to be born of her by the Holy Spirit. Matthew has an annunciation too. But Matthew does not speak of an annunciation to Mary; he speaks of an annunciation to Joseph. Of course, these do not contradict each other. There could well have been an annunciation to Mary and a second annunciation to Joseph. In fact, we believe that is exactly what happened. But if Matthew and Luke were getting together to compose their gospels and were working up a story between them, that is the kind of apparent contradiction they would have eliminated. Luke would have said, "Matthew, that is a very good story that you've got of an angel appearing to Joseph, but in my account I've got him appearing to Mary. We can't have that. Let's decide who it's going to be. If you're set on your way, I'll go with you. But if not, let's flip a denarius and decide." They would probably include only one, or both annunciations in both narratives, if they were working together.

Here is another apparent contradiction. Luke tells about shepherds coming to worship the infant Christ. But what does

Matthew have? Matthew has wise men, kings of the east. If they were operating in collusion, I can imagine Matthew's saying to Luke, "Luke, that is a very poignant, simple, touching story that you've created. But you have missed the great theology that I'm trying to communicate by my story; I want to indicate that even the Gentile kings come and bow down to Jesus." Luke would say, "That's a good point, but Christianity is still a downtrodden religion, and we won't see many kings being converted. Wouldn't it be better if we talked about shepherds and forgot the kings?" These men would have worked out one story or the other, if they were working together.

There are more examples. Luke indicates that Joseph and Mary came from Nazareth and says very clearly that they went up to Bethlehem only because of the decree from Caesar Augustus that all the world should be registered. But Matthew begins with Mary and Joseph in Bethlehem. In Matthew there is no reference to Nazareth until the end of chapter 2, where we are told that after Mary and Joseph had come back from Egypt they decided not to return to Bethlehem but went on to Nazareth in order that the Old Testament prophecy "he will be called a Nazarene" might be fulfilled. These are not in conflict. We understand how they can be put together. But they are the kind of thing that careful authors such as Matthew and Luke would have eliminated if they were working in collusion.

What about the second possibility, that they invented the stories separately? Matthew was sitting in his little office in Jerusalem and Luke was sitting in his little office somewhere else, and they did not have anything to do with one another. They did not even know about one another's stories. Each just said, "I am going to make up something that will really be a good story." If that were the case, you would have discrepancies, but you would not have the kind of obvious agreement the two accounts have. There are differences, but there is no mistaking the fact that we are dealing with the same story. There are the same characters: Mary, Joseph, and the baby. Moreover, they are the same people in both accounts and not merely the same names. Matthew's Joseph is Luke's Joseph, and Luke's Mary is Matthew's Mary. Again, the great event, the birth of Jesus Christ by miraculous means, is identical.

Where does that leave us? Well, if you eliminate the possibility that the stories were made up in collusion and the possibility that they were made up separately, the only other possibility is that they were not made up at all but rather are reflections of true events as their authors knew them. They bear the kind of superficial differences but underlying unity you find when independent witnesses testify to an event.

THE FLOW OF HISTORY

When we put these events together we have a long but consistent history. First, Zechariah was informed concerning the birth of John the Baptist (Luke 1:5–25). The annunciation to Zechariah was followed by the annunciation to Mary, an account parallel to the first (Luke 1:26–38). Third, Mary visited Elizabeth (Luke 1:39–56). That is entirely understandable. Mary was told by the angel that she was to conceive and give birth to a child without a human father. She believed God was going to do that, but could not communicate this mystery to another living soul. Yet since the angel had said

that God was going to bless Mary's relative with a child conceived in old age, Mary instinctively recognized that if there
was anybody who could understand what was happening to
her, it was Elizabeth. So off she went! She stayed there three
months. At last we have the return of Mary to Nazareth and,
sometime in that period, the birth of John the Baptist (Luke
1:57–80).

Matthew picks up the story at that point. He says nothing of the events that have gone before, but they are necessary to understand fully what happened next. Matthew tells
of the discovery of Mary's condition (Matthew 1:18–25).
Joseph was tempted to divorce her quietly. But there was
then a third annunciation (which in Matthew is the first)
in which an angel explained to Joseph what was happening.
Joseph believed the angel just as Mary had believed the
angel, and Joseph then took Mary under his protection to
shield her from the danger she would be exposed to if he
had divorced her or simply left her alone in her condition
in the world.

Luke continues the story, telling of the journey to Bethlehem, which explains how the couple got there (Luke 2:1–5).
Matthew and Luke both naturally tell about the birth of Jesus
(Matthew 1:25; Luke 2:6–7). Then Luke picks up again, telling
of the visit of the shepherds (Luke 2:8–20), the circumcision
of Jesus at Bethlehem eight days after His birth (Luke 2:21),
the presentation in the Temple on the fortieth day, including the incidents connected with that presentation (Simeon,
Anna, and others, who looked for the redemption in Jerusalem, recognized that the Savior had arrived), and the return
to Bethlehem (Luke 2:22–40).

Matthew now tells about the visit of the magi (Matthew 2:1–12), the flight to Egypt (Matthew 2:13–18), and finally the return to Nazareth, which is also told by Luke, though he does not relate the other instances (Matthew 2:19–23; Luke 2:39).

What do we have in these accounts? We have independent but complementary narrations of what happened. Each tells different parts of the narrative, but the parts fit together into a whole because what is being related is fact. We found when we studied Luke's account separately that it was credible. The only thing we must add is that, although these events are fully historical, they are nevertheless also supernatural. For here the supernatural enters into history by the grace of God.

5

THE GENEALOGIES

NEWSWEEK MAGAZINE MARKED the end of 1979 with a cover story attacking the historical Jesus and the historicity of the biblical accounts. The article was based on the higher criticism of the New Testament and was written by a reporter who understood very little about it. The impression given was that none of the gospels bears any relationship to eyewitness accounts of the life, death, and resurrection of Jesus Christ, and as a result they are almost entirely invention. Very little can be known about the historical Jesus.

When I was a student I took that kind of article more seriously than I do now, because when you are a student you cannot afford not to take your professors' theories seriously. Today I am far less inclined to give serious consideration to them. In fact, I am convinced that this approach is utterly wrong. If it is true that the gospels bear no relationship to eyewitness accounts, then it is possible to think of the stories of Jesus as inventions expressing the subjective experience of the writers. But if, by contrast, as the gospels themselves claim, they are the work of eyewitnesses who wrote about the things they knew, then this whole approach to the Bible simply has to be thrown out.

I introduce our study of the genealogies of Christ in this way because what I have been saying about the birth narratives in Matthew and Luke is entirely contrary to critical opinion. If, as I have argued, the accounts are not invented in collusion or separately, then they are not invented at all but are works of men writing about things they knew. They are factual and can be believed completely.

PROBLEM OF THE GENEALOGIES

Having said that, however, let me say that there is one part of the narratives, both in Matthew and Luke, that gives exceptional difficulty, the genealogies. It does not require a great New Testament scholar or even a very astute reader of the New Testament to recognize that, when we read the genealogy as Matthew gives it and contrast it with the genealogy as Luke gives it, we are dealing at least in portions with two entirely different things. That would be all right if we were dealing with the descent of two different people. But the genealogies both speak expressly of Joseph, the husband of Mary, of whom Jesus Christ was born, and they differ in their listing of ancestors between Joseph and David. On the surface at least that seems to be so great a contradiction that we might assume that the writers simply did not know what they were talking about.

Regardless of this obvious difficulty, the genealogies do at least give testimony to the virgin birth. At the very end of the genealogy in Matthew (Matthew 1:16), Matthew writes of "Jacob the father of Joseph, the husband of Mary, of whom was born Jesus, who is called Christ." Matthew does not say that Joseph was the father of Jesus. We find the same thing in Luke, though Luke does it differently. Luke says, "Now Jesus himself was about thirty years old when he began his ministry. He was the son, so it was thought, of Joseph, the son of Heli," and so on (Luke 3:23). Luke is giving a different genealogy, but he is nevertheless testifying to the virgin birth. He is saying that Joseph was thought to be the father of Jesus but in point of fact was not the father. He was only the husband of Mary, who was the mother of Jesus.

What are the difficulties? Well, Matthew's genealogy begins with Abraham and moves forward in history to Christ. It traces Abraham's descendants through fourteen generations to David, David's descendants through fourteen generations to the Babylonian captivity, then the later descendants through fourteen more generations up to "Jacob the father of Joseph, the husband of Mary, of whom was born Jesus, who is called Christ." Luke, on the other hand, moves backward. He begins with Joseph and goes back through David, to Abraham—and then even back beyond Abraham to Adam, who, he says, was "the son of God."

Two of Luke's sections present no problem. His final section—from Abraham to Adam—does not occur in Matthew. So there is no basis for comparison. His second section—from David to Abraham—is also free of problems because it corresponds to the genealogy we find in Matthew.

The difficulty comes in Luke's first section. For Luke traces Joseph's descendants back to David through Nathan, one of

David's sons, while Matthew traces what is apparently the same line of descent through Solomon, another of David's sons. Consequently, in this section of the genealogies all the names are different.

The fact that these are two separate lines is no problem. We can understand how two different sons of David would give birth to two different family trees. The difficulty is that Matthew and Luke both claim Joseph as a descendant of their particular trees. Luke says that Joseph was the son of Heli (3:23), Matthew says that Joseph was the son of Jacob (1:16), and both apparently cannot be true.

MACHEN'S SOLUTION

Several solutions to this problem have been offered. J. Gresham Machen analyzes the problem with customary thoroughness and suggests that these are indeed both genealogies of Joseph but that Matthew gives what Machen calls the "legal" descendants of David, that is, the line that actually sat upon the throne or would have, had it continued, and that Luke gives the actual "paternal" line that produced Joseph.

He explains the different fathers of Joseph by saying that Matthew's line does not necessarily indicate literal father-son relationships but only a list of heirs to the throne, whatever their relationships to their immediate predecessors may have been. In this view, Heli would be Joseph's literal father. But Jacob (who presumably had no sons to follow him) would have been Joseph's immediate predecessor in the "legal" line.[1]

---

1. J. Gresham Machen, *The Virgin Birth of Christ* (1930; reprint, London: James Clarke, 1958), pp. 202–9.

That makes good sense, for Matthew is certainly talking about heirs to the throne. His is a Jewish gospel. Moreover, he constructs his genealogy from David onward, asking, "Who is the next heir?" By contrast, Luke is interested in actual paternity. So he constructs his genealogy from Joseph back to David, asking, "Who was so-and-so's father?"

Machen writes, "Reconciliation [of the two accounts] might conceivably be effected in a number of different ways. But on the whole we are inclined to think that the true key to a solution to the problem (however the solution may run in detail) is to be found in the fact that Matthew, in an intentionally incomplete way, gives a list of incumbents (actually or potential) of the kingly Davidic throne, whereas Luke traces the descent of Joseph back through Nathan to David. Thus the genealogies cannot properly be used to exhibit contradiction between the Matthaean and the Lukan accounts of the birth and infancy of our Lord."[2]

That is a very good theory and may well be right, but I have one problem with it. According to Machen's theory the loose genealogy is Matthew's genealogy. It is the one that is not necessarily talking about a literal descent from father to son. Luke's genealogy is talking about fatherhood and sonship. But it is a striking thing, if that is the case, that it is Matthew who stresses the descent from father to son by use of the word *begat*— "Abraham begat Isaac, and Isaac begat Jacob" (KJV; NIV says "was the father of")—while Luke uses a looser way of indicating the relationship, saying simply "of the" (NIV translates "son of"). If Luke was talking about strict paternity, he is the one who should have used the word *begat*, and if Matthew was not talking about it, he should have used the looser form.

2. Ibid., p. 209.

JOSEPH'S AND MARY'S LINES

In my judgment there is a better solution, in which the two lines are viewed as the lines of Joseph and Mary respectively, each thereby being identified as a descendant of King David. That was the view of Bernhard Weiss and of Scotland's James Orr.[3] But it has received classic expression in more recent writing by Donald Grey Barnhouse, from which I quote.

> There [are] two genealogies. The lines run parallel from Abraham to David, but then Matthew comes down to Jesus by way of Solomon the son of David. In other words, the two genealogies are the lines of two brothers and the children become cousins. When I state that Luke's genealogy is that of the Virgin Mary and Matthew's genealogy is that of Joseph, I am not merely following the persistent tradition of the earthly church, as Dr. James Orr states it, but I am setting forth the only explanation that will fit the facts. The whole point of the difference is that Solomon's line was the royal line and Nathan's line was the legal line.
>
> For example, the former king of England had an older brother, now the Duke of Windsor, who had a prior claim to the throne of Britain. Suppose that Windsor had been the father of a son by a real queen before he abdicated. It can readily be seen that such a child might be a strong pretender to the throne in case there was no other heir apparent. George VI is in the royal line for he has reigned; any children of Windsor might claim to be in a legal line. Nathan was the older brother of Solomon, but the younger brother took the

3. Bernhard Weiss, "Die Evangelien des Markus und Lukus," in H. A. W. Meyer, ed., *Kritisch-exegetischer Kommentar über das Neue Testament* (Göttingen: Vandenhoeck & Ruprecht, 1901), p. 331; and James Orr, "The Virgin Birth of Christ" (1907), in *The Fundamentals*, ed. R. A. Torrey, A. C. Dixon et al. (Grand Rapids: Baker, 1972), 2: 247–60.

throne. Nathan's line ran on through the years, and ultimately produced the Virgin Mary. Solomon's line ran on through the years and ultimately produced Joseph. Matthew does not say that Joseph begat Jesus, but that he was the husband of Mary, of whom was born Jesus (Matt. 1:16). And Luke uses a word for son that includes what we should call a son-in-law.

But the greatest proof of all lies in one of the names in the account of Matthew: the name Jechonias. It is that name that furnishes the reason for the inclusion of the genealogy of Jesus' step-father, for it proves that Joseph could not have been the father of Jesus, or if he had been, that Jesus could not have been the Messiah. In the use of that name is conclusive evidence that Jesus is the son of Mary and not the son of Joseph. Jechonias was accursed of God with a curse that took the throne away from any of his descendants. "Thus saith the Lord," we read in Jeremiah 22:30, "write yet this man childless, a man that shall not prosper in his days: for no man of his seed shall prosper, sitting upon the throne of David, and ruling any more in Judah." Not one of the seven sons (1 Chron. 3:17, 18) of this man ever possessed the throne. No carnal son of this man could have been king because of the curse of God. If Jesus had been the son of Joseph, He would have been accursed and could never have been the Messiah.

On the other hand, the line of Nathan was not the royal line. A son of Heli would have faced the fact that there was a regal line that would have contested any claim that came from the line of Nathan. How was the dilemma solved? It was solved in a manner that is so simple that it is the utter confusion of the agnostics who seek to tear the Bible to pieces. The answer is this: The line that had no curse upon it produced Heli and his daughter the Virgin Mary and her Son Jesus Christ. He is therefore eligible by the line of Nathan and exhausts that line. The line that had a curse on it produced Joseph, exhausts the line of Solomon, for Joseph's other children now have an older brother who, legally, by adoption, is the royal heir. How can the title be free in any case? A curse on one line and the lack of reigning royalty in the other.

But when God the Holy Spirit begat the Lord Jesus in the womb of the Virgin without any use of a human father, the child that was born was the seed of David according to the flesh. And when Joseph married Mary and took the unborn child under his protecting care, giving Him the title that had come down to Him through His ancestor Solomon, the Lord Jesus became the legal Messiah, the royal Messiah, the uncursed Messiah, the true Messiah, the only possible Messiah. The lines are exhausted. Any man that ever comes into this world professing to fulfill the conditions will be a liar and the child of the Devil.[4]

ALL SCRIPTURE PROFITABLE

There are a few conclusions. First, this problem teaches us how to deal with difficulties in Scripture. When we come to a problem like this on which sometimes even conservative scholars are not agreed, we think it unsolvable. But as we work on it and think about it, we see how the difficulties can be resolved. That encourages us to be patient when we deal with other difficulties.

Years ago a Bible teacher was riding on a train and went into the dining car for dinner. A man sat down across from

---

4. Donald Grey Barnhouse, *Man's Ruin*, vol. 1 of *Expositions of Bible Doctrines* (Grand Rapids: Eerdmans, 1952), pp. 45–47. Used by permission.

him who, as it turned out, was an atheist. Finding that his companion was a Bible teacher, the atheist began to rehearse the difficulties he perceived to be in Scripture. He gave one after the other, but the man who was being attacked went right on eating. He was eating New England cod, a very bony fish, and as he ate he pushed the bones aside. Finally the atheist said, "Well, what do you do with that? What do you do with all those difficulties in the Bible?"

The Bible teacher said, "I do with the difficulties just as I am doing with this cod. I eat the meat, and I put the bones aside for some fool to choke on."

A story like that can be overdone if we suppose by it that we do not have to grapple with difficulties. We do. We have to give the best possible answers we can give. But if, in a given period of history with a limited amount of knowledge, we come to a difficulty we cannot resolve, it is certainly not dishonesty but merely a mark of humility to push the problem aside temporarily until more data comes in.

The second lesson is patience in waiting for the second coming of Christ. Down through the years of Old Testament history men and women looked forward to the coming of the Messiah. Every child of David was a potential Messiah, and the people kept their genealogies straight because they wanted to know who might possibly reign upon the throne. Generation after generation went by, yet the Messiah did not come. It was only after a long wait that Jesus was at last born in Bethlehem, and those who had been waiting, people like Simeon and Anna, saw Him and rejoiced at His coming. In a similar way, in our day the second coming of the Lord Jesus Christ seems delayed, and the skeptics say, "Where is this 'coming' he promised? Ever since our fathers died, everything goes on as it has since the beginning of creation" (2 Peter 3:4). But all things have not continued unchanged from the beginning. Christ came once, and He will soon come again. Knowing this, we should be patient and trust God to work in His own way and time.

The final conclusion is the value of all Scripture. Second Timothy 3:16 says, "All Scripture is . . . useful." That includes even the genealogies! We read them and sometimes say, "What possible value can these things have?" Yet they do have value, and even these problem genealogies and their solution have been used to bring people to faith in Christ.

Rom Blankley, a former area director for Campus Crusade for Christ, was walking through the Student Union of the University of Pennsylvania one day when he saw a student reading a Bible. He remembered Philip's approach to the Ethiopian. So he walked over to him and said, "Do you understand what you are reading?"

The student replied, "No, as a matter of fact, I don't. I'm reading the genealogies of Jesus in Matthew and Luke, and I don't understand them because they seem to be different." Blankley sat down and explained the genealogies much as I have done here, and as a result of that explanation the young man came to faith in Jesus Christ as his Savior.

The world has no use for Christ, so it is not surprising that it has no use for Christ's words. But we who know the power of Christ know the power of the Word as well, and we should not be afraid to study and proclaim it. The Spirit of Christ will work through it to bring many to the Savior.

6

THE VIRGIN BIRTH AND CHRISTIAN FAITH

THE FIRST TIME I PREACHED a series on the virgin birth of Christ, at Christmastime, a student came up to me afterward and was very excited about it. He had never heard a message, let alone a series of messages, on the virgin birth, and it struck him not only as novel but as very significant to hear this. "You know," he said, "I have never heard a message on the virgin birth. Why do you suppose that is?"

I began to mull over that question and ask myself why the virgin birth is so little spoken of. One answer might be that the virgin birth is not something that is spoken of widely in the New Testament. Another might be simple unbelief. But as I thought about it further, it struck me that the primary reason the virgin birth is not preached on more often is that on the surface at least it is hard to see how it is relevant to the Christian faith. It might be taught in Scripture. Evangelicals would certainly confess that it is true. But it is hard to see how it relates to other Christian doctrines and how it has bearing upon the Christian life.

Does it have bearing? We are encouraged to think so by 2 Timothy 3:16, which tells us that "*all* Scripture is God-breathed and is useful" (emphasis added). If that is true, then the Scriptures dealing with the virgin birth are also useful, and it is simply up to us to find out in what ways.

Our View of Scripture

Why is the virgin birth important? It seems to me that it is important for our view of Scripture, particularly in the area of biblical authority. It is quite easy to see how that is the case. The Bible teaches the virgin birth. So the question the reader must face is whether the Bible is truthful when it teaches it. Can the Bible be trusted at this point and therefore at other points as well?

What we have in our day is not so much an outright denial of the authority of Scripture by theology professors and ministers—because we do not live in a day of brave men who take a position and follow it through radically. We deal in compromise and half-truths.

What we have in our day is a view that usually goes by the name of partial inspiration or partial authority. It sees Scripture as true, but not throughout. It is true, but only partially. Therefore, the task of the scholar, preacher, or Christian layman is to read the Bible and discern which parts are truthful. Unfortunately, when one approaches the Bible like that, one is on dangerous ground. Because, having given up authority of the whole, it is almost impossible to resist the trend to give up more and more until one comes eventually to doubt whether God has spoken in Scripture at all or whether the Bible has more authority than any other human document.

That is the point Harold Lindsell has tried to make in his book *The Battle for the Bible*.[1] He says there is a sequence in that approach that goes something like this: A person starts out with a high view of Scripture, perhaps because it is what he was taught in a fundamental church or home. But then, through exposure to the critical biblical views of the day, he finds he has increasing difficulty answering certain problems, and because he does not want to look foolish in the eyes of others he begins to retreat from a commitment to a totally reliable Scripture to a view that in his mind preserves the essence of biblical truthfulness but yields at the point of difficulty. Usually he claims that the Bible is inerrant in matters of faith and practice (that is, doctrine and life) but not necessarily in matters of history or science.

When our creeds say that the Bible is the only infallible rule of faith and practice, they mean that the Word of God, being the Word of God, is our infallible guide in all things. But people like this mean that it is only partially authoritative. They mean, "We can yield in matters of history or science because that doesn't matter. So long as the Bible can be trusted to tell us what to believe and how to conduct our lives, we're all right."

But then, as Lindsell points out, having yielded the authority of the Bible in all areas and fallen back to a defense of its inerrancy in just these two limited areas, the next step is to yield the authority of the Bible in the area of practice.

1. Harold Lindsell, *The Battle for the Bible* (Grand Rapids: Zondervan, 1976).

A person says, "Well, we still believe the Christian doctrines, but in terms of how we live and how we conduct the affairs of our churches it is not really necessary to be bound by what the Bible says because, after all, we know that the Bible is not inerrant in matters of history and science and there is no reason to think that it is inerrant in matters of conduct either." The next thing to go is doctrine, and soon the person has retreated to partial agnosticism or perhaps to no faith at all.

A number of years ago a book was compiled by a professor from a well-known evangelical seminary. It was called *Biblical Authority*. You would think that a book called *Biblical Authority* would be about the authority of the Bible, but the message of the book was actually that a person can have biblical authority without inerrancy. It says that the Bible can be wrong in certain points and still be authoritative. In response, the International Council on Biblical Inerrancy put together an answer called, significantly enough, *The Foundation of Biblical Authority*, because it was our intention to show that inerrancy is a necessary foundation for preserving Bible truth.[2]

Let us assume for the sake of argument that the Bible can be in error in certain facts of history or science, and perhaps even in the matter of the virgin birth, but that it is not in error when it deals with faith and practice. The question I ask is, How are we going to distinguish between these areas?

You say, "That's easy! One area concerns doctrine and morals; the other concerns history." But, you see, the distinct feature of Christianity over against the other world religions is that Christianity is historical. When we talk about Chris-

2. James Montgomery Boice, ed., *The Foundation of Biblical Authority* (Grand Rapids: Zondervan, 1978).

tian doctrine, arguing that God has revealed Himself in Jesus Christ and that Jesus Christ died for our sins, what are we doing but talking history? We are saying that God has revealed Himself in a real man, Jesus of Nazareth, in a real place and time, and that God accomplished something in Christ in history that could not have been accomplished in any other way. History and doctrine are interwoven.

Moreover, if we find ourselves in the position of distinguishing between what is inerrant and therefore authoritative and what is errant and therefore not authoritative, the real authority is not Scripture's (where God speaks to the human mind and conscience) but our own. For we, not God, are deciding what we will believe.

When we ask whether the doctrine of the virgin birth is true or false, we are asking far more than simply, Did Jesus have a virgin birth? We are asking, What is my view of Scripture and, therefore, what is my view of Christianity?

In the ultimate analysis the choice boils down to this: It is either the whole Bible and whole Christianity, or it is no Bible and no Christianity. I do not mean that people who abandon belief in the Bible's total inerrancy necessarily end up with no doctrine at all or totally deny Jesus Christ. That is not true. Not all of us operate consistently on the basis of our presuppositions. But there is always that danger.

OUR WORLD VIEW

Second, the virgin birth is important in regard to our world view. When I speak of a world view I mean a total world philosophy. The most important issue in philosophy is whether we are living in a closed universe or an open universe. When we look about at the visible universe, when we see matter and the laws that govern it, the basic question is whether that is all there is. If it is, we have a closed universe. That is the dominant view of our time. On the other hand, when we look at the universe of things and ideas, do we confess that we are not dealing with a closed universe but with a universe in which God lies above and beyond what we see? That is an open universe, and that is the Bible's view.

Apart from Christianity, our culture is moving increasingly toward a closed-universe view. That is the meaning, I believe, of some of the science-fiction films that are now so popular. In these films, no mater how great or fantastic the ideas and experiences may seem to be, in the final analysis the things discovered are only material and explainable.

Star Trek: the Motion Picture, for example, is about a power's coming toward earth and about beings from earth who are going out to intercept it. This thing expresses its mission as a quest "for its creator." You expect its creator to be God. But when the adventurers get down to finding out what it really is, they find that it is a machine that has been made by human beings. So, in this case, the people themselves become creators. They become gods.

Christianity says something radically different. And if you do not understand that, you do not understand Christianity at all. We live in a world that is increasingly materialistic. Often we cannot see beyond the bounds of the material. But Christianity says that there is something beyond the material. That something is God, and God is the Creator of the material. Furthermore, He is the one who has revealed Himself to us in Jesus of Nazareth. The virgin birth testifies to that reality.

Drop away from science for a minute and fall back to Christian terminology. How in Christian terminology can you test whether a person really believes in an open system? You say, "Let's test him at the point of the deity of Jesus Christ. Let's ask, 'Do you believe in the deity of Jesus Christ?'"

The person answers, "Yes."

"Do you believe that Jesus is the Son of God?"

The person says yes again.

Well, you say, "that's wonderful! He's a believer!" But that is not necessarily the case. Not today. Because the words *deity*, *Son of God*, and even *God* itself can be ambivalent. The affirmation may merely mean "I believe Jesus is the Son of God in the same way that I'm a son of God or you're a son of God." That does not mean a great deal.

The point I am making is that the virgin birth is not like that. The virgin birth tells us that God invaded history. That is unlike anything else that has ever happened. None of us has ever had a similar experience. So if the virgin birth is true, it means that there is a God, that He is beyond the system we see, and, furthermore, that He is concerned about us and has demonstrated that concern through the incarnation. In that way the virgin birth is vitally important for our world view.

OUR VIEW OF JESUS

Third, the virgin birth is important to our view of Jesus. The way we should approach the virgin birth is not by saying, "If Christ was virgin born, then He must be the Son of God, and therefore what He said can be believed and what He did can be trusted. He is our Savior." I do not think that is the best approach because doing that would make it possible, I suppose, to deal with the virgin birth without bringing in any other necessary aspects of Christology. The way I think we should come at it is this: We take the person of Christ presented in the gospels, and we ask, "Is Jesus a mere man—talented, of great ability, perhaps far beyond any others of His time, but still a man? Or is He more than a man? Is He God in addition to being man?"

If we answer that question as Christians do, on the side of the deity, then we look back to the virgin birth and find that the doctrine is entirely appropriate within that context. We may not understand it. In physical terms we cannot say how it is possible for a human being to be born without a human father. Nevertheless, if Jesus is more than mere man, if Jesus is God, the virgin birth is not at all unreasonable or inappropriate.

That is what theologians have recognized. B. B. Warfield said, "He who casts himself upon Jesus as his divine Redeemer, will find the fact of the Virgin Birth of this Savior not only consonant with his faith and an aid to it, but a postulate of it without which he would be puzzled and confused."[3]

THE VIRGIN BIRTH ITSELF

Finally, the virgin birth is important in itself. For one thing, it fixes the time of the incarnation. Why does that matter? It matters in terms of the various views of the incarnation that have existed in Christian theology. In the early days of the church some

3. Benjamin B. Warfield, "The Supernatural Birth of Jesus," in *Biblical and Theological Studies* (Philadelphia: Presbyterian and Reformed, 1968), p. 168.

thought that the heavenly Christ came upon Jesus of Nazareth, a mere human being, at a later point in His human life. Some taught that it was at Jesus' baptism. One of the quirks of this particular theology was that God cannot suffer. So it was supposed that the heavenly Christ left Jesus just before His crucifixion.

By contrast, the virgin birth tells us that there was never a moment in the human life of Jesus Christ, going back to the very moment of His conception, when Jesus was not God. He was always God. He was the God-man from the beginning.

Again, the virgin birth is important in itself because it shows us how Christ was free from sin. There is a difficulty in talking about this because there is much about the virgin birth of which we are ignorant. We do not know how Jesus was conceived. We do not even know how sin is passed on from one human being to another. Nevertheless, there is a sense in which the virgin birth teaches us how Jesus was free from sin.

According to one theology, none of that means anything because sin is not passed on. Each person is a unique individual who sins for himself, and one person's sin never affects another. In such a system, the matter of the virgin birth means little because Jesus could be born in a natural way and just choose not to sin. He did not need to have a virgin birth. In a better theological system (Augustine's), that does not work. Because, as Augustine rightly saw, sin is also a collective thing whereby we are condemned for the sin of Adam (as well as our own sin), and the condemnation of Adam passes upon the race because of our biological connection to him. According to this system, the virgin birth is very important, for it shows that the Lord did not inherit a sinful nature or the curse that comes to Adam's descendants.

A Necessary Doctrine

When you get to the bottom line, it is not a question of whether one can be a Christian and deny the virgin birth. That is to ask, in effect, "How little can one believe and still be a Christian?" I suppose one can believe very little and still be a Christian. One need only know that he or she is a sinner and that Jesus, the Son of God, died in his or her place. Basically that is all one has to know. But we are on the wrong track when we ask the question like that. The real question is, Is the virgin birth essential, not to be a Christian, but for Christianity? And at that point we answer with an emphatic "Yes! It certainly is!"

Christianity is not just a collection of random truths, any one of which could be dropped with little harm. It is truth, and truth is a whole. Consequently, a diminution at any point inevitably affects the rest, given enough time. When we begin to drop this doctrine or that doctrine, even though we cannot see at the time how it will affect the rest, it nevertheless does affect the rest. And Christianity and ourselves are poorer for the loss. What we want to ask is, Does the Word of God teach this truth? For if it does, we want to believe it and turn to God for ever increasing understanding.

Anselm of Canterbury had a wonderful expression in this regard: *Fides quarens intellectum*, meaning "Faith in search of understanding." That is what we want. We want to believe and then go on to the fullness of that understanding imparted through careful study of the Word of God.

THE
FIRST
CHRISTMAS

7

THE KING IN A MANGER

EVERY PERSON has a birthday, and most birthdays are remembered at least by the person himself and usually by his immediate family. But no birthday has ever been remembered so widely as the birthday of the Lord Jesus Christ.

We know that there is no real evidence that He was born on December 25. In fact, the one small bit of evidence we do have goes against that date. We are told that an announcement of His birth was made to shepherds when they were in the fields with their sheep, and that is normally true only during the spring and summer months, between late March and September. Actually, we observe the birth of Jesus on the day we do because this date was established by consensus during the first Christian centuries and has been preserved by tradition. But that is relatively unimportant. The important thing is that Jesus was born, and the interesting fact is that so many remember His birth.

Why is this? It is true that many remember the birth of Christ because they are Christians and therefore love and cherish Him. But millions of others are not Christians and yet also celebrate Christmas. Why has the birth of this one man so seized upon the minds and imaginations of men and women?

CHRISTMAS PARADOXES

Answers to that question are found in the paradoxes of the Christmas story, one of which we want to look at in detail.

One obvious paradox is of purity in the account of the birth of a child to an unwed mother. The birth of a child to a girl who is not married is not surprising or even remarkable, though it is tragic. It is a story known to any preacher—the girl, quite often deeply distressed; the parents, frantic with grief and indecision. But the tone of distress and grief we know is not the tone of this story. Rather, there is purity: the purity of Mary who, we are told, was troubled by the angel's announcement and asked in innocence, "How will this be . . . since I am a virgin?" (Luke 1:34); and the purity of Joseph, who was not the father but who believed the announcement of the angel and so shielded Mary by marrying her, though he did not have intercourse with her until after Jesus was born.

A second paradox follows that one. It is also a story of joy in what would normally be a tragedy. Under normal circumstances Mary would have been in danger of vicious public exposure and even death, for stoning was the penalty prescribed for fornication in Israel. She would have been distraught and in anguish. Yet when Mary came to her cousin Elizabeth, to whom she had gone to share her unbelievable news, Elizabeth at once broke forth in praise to God and in ascriptions of blessings on Mary, and Mary responded with that great hymn of praise known as the Magnificat.

There are other contrasts in this story. There is the announcement of the birth of the baby to shepherds, those from the lowest levels of ancient Jewish society, by angels who are certainly figures of great stature and glory. There is the neglect of Jesus by His own people, while Gentile wise men came to worship Him. Even the baby is a paradox. For unlike other babies, who are born to live, this child was born to die.

And yet, in this great story so filled with paradoxes, there is one paradox that stands out above the rest, and perhaps more than any other commends the account to many people. It is that the one born in such lowly surroundings—in a stable, of poor parents, laid in an animal's manger—was nevertheless the God of glory, whose splendor before the incarnation surpassed that even of those heavenly beings who announced His birth to the shepherds. Here is a baby. But He is the King of kings and Lord of lords. He is God in a stable. He is the supreme potentate of the universe among His own lowly cattle.

That is the paradox of the incarnation: Immanuel!

CAESAR AND CHRIST

That paradox did not escape the biblical writers. In fact, as we study the Christmas narratives, we soon find that not only was it known to them, but it was actually emphasized. We see this clearly in Luke's gospel in the best known verses of the story (vv. 1–7). It is pointed up in three ways.

First, there is a reference to Augustus Caesar, who was in that day the supreme and powerful leader of the world. Prior to the reign of Augustus the empire had been in great turmoil. There had been the advance of Julius Caesar over the Rubicon, which led to the death of the Republic and in time to Caesar's own death by assassination. That was followed by the civil wars in which Anthony and Octavius defeated Brutus and Cassius. Then there was war between Anthony and the quickly ascending Augustus.

In all there were twenty years of turmoil, and it was only at the end of that period that Augustus, now the sole ruler of the empire, established peace. Moreover, it was not only in civil war that Augustus proved victorious. He also conducted wars on the various borders of the empire against invaders and on the seas against pirates. He established the Pax Romana. To a degree he even restored the Republic, for under his reign the senate, magistrates, and assembly resumed their ancient functions. Rome prospered, and wealth and glory flowed freely into Caesar's capital.

That is the individual Luke mentions as he begins his account of Christ's birth. So to us, and certainly to all who lived in Luke's time, the contrast between the power, fame, and glory of Augustus and the weakness, obscurity, and humility of the babe of Bethlehem is obvious.

Second, there is a downward progression in the status of the five characters mentioned in these verses. We notice that it is not just Caesar who is mentioned. Quirinius, the governor of Syria, is also mentioned, and so are Joseph and Mary. At the peak of the social structure is Caesar. Quirinius is farther down, yet still a man of prestige and power. Joseph is lower, for he is just a working man from Nazareth in Galilee. After that comes Mary, a woman and therefore even farther down the scale according to the values of that day. At the very end and at the lowest possible point on the social scale is Jesus. He is just an infant, the poorest of the poor, as far from Caesar as anyone could possibly be. Yet He was infinitely above Caesar both in the majesty of His person and in dignity.

Third, we note the details of Christ's birth. These are humble, as I have already indicated. On the night the angels appeared near Bethlehem, Caesar would have been sleeping in Rome on a golden bed beneath sheets of fine linen. He would have been attended by servants, protected by the Praetorian guard and the many Roman legions. By contrast, the babe was wrapped in swaddling clothes and placed in a manger. His attendants were beasts.

EIGHT CONTRASTS

This paradox has undoubtedly commended the story to many generations of people, but we have not exhausted it yet. For according to the full teaching of the Word of God, Jesus descended from the peak of glory to this lowly position in order that He might raise us from our lowly position to His glory. The apostle Paul mentions this in 2 Corinthians 8:9 when he writes, "For you know the grace of our Lord Jesus Christ, that though he was rich, yet for your sakes he became poor, so that you through his poverty might become rich."

That reminds me of a message on the "Contrasts of Christmas" by Donald Grey Barnhouse on "The Bible Study Hour." It is of interest here because each of the eight contrasts developed by Barnhouse illustrates this central paradox.

First, Barnhouse compared Luke 2:11 with John 1:12. Both deal with birth. In the first verse the angels are speaking to the shepherds. They are saying, "Today in the town of David a Savior has been born to you; he is Christ the Lord." In the second verse, John is writing of the new birth that comes to those who believe on Jesus. "To all who received him, to those who believed in his name, he gave the right to become children of God." The point is that Jesus underwent a human birth so that we who believe on Him might have a heavenly birth.

Second, there is a contrast between Luke 2:7 and John 14:2. In Luke we are told that Mary laid the newborn Christ "in a manger, because there was no room for them in the inn." In John we read, "In my Father's house are many rooms; if it were not so, I would have told you. I am going there to prepare a place for you." We note that Jesus took His place in a manger in a stable, so that we might have heavenly mansions.

Third, we take Matthew 2:11 and place it alongside Galatians 3:26. "On coming to the house, they saw the child with his mother Mary." Then, "You are all sons of God through faith in Christ Jesus." Here we learn that Jesus became a member

of a human family so that we might become members of the
family of God.

Fourth, we compare Luke 2:51 with Galatians 5:1. Luke
2:51 is written of the days of Christ's childhood, of which it
is said, "Then he went down to Nazareth with them and was
obedient to them." By contrast, Galatians 5:1 reads, "It is for
freedom that Christ has set us free. Stand firm, then, and do
not let yourselves be burdened again by a yoke of slavery." Jesus
made Himself subject to others so that we, through the power
of His Spirit at work within us, might be made free.

Fifth, in Philippians 2:6–7 we are told that Jesus, though
"being in very nature God, did not consider equality with God
something to be grasped, but made himself nothing [that is,
emptied himself of his divine glory], taking the very nature
of a servant"; whereas in 1 Peter 5:4 we are reminded that
"when the Chief Shepherd appears, you will receive the crown
of glory that will never fade away." Jesus laid His glory aside
that we might receive glory.

Sixth, Matthew 8:20 says that during the days of His
earthly ministry the Lord was so poor that He had "no place
to lay his head." We, on the other hand, have "through his
poverty" been made "rich" (2 Corinthians 8:9).

The seventh contrast is between Luke 2:16 and Luke 15:10.
In the first verse Jesus, on the occasion of His coming to earth,
was welcomed by shepherds: "So they hurried off and found
Mary and Joseph, and the baby, who was lying in the manger."
In the second verse we are told that we, on the occasion of
our second birth, are rejoiced over by angels: "In the same
way, I tell you, there is rejoicing in the presence of the angels
of God over one sinner who repents."

Finally, we are told in Matthew 2:13 that Herod, that wicked and deceitful king, sought the young child "to destroy it." Jesus was pursued by this evil ruler so that, as Hebrews 2:14 and 15 tell us, He might "destroy" that far more dangerous and evil ruler who pursues us. "Since the children have flesh and blood, he too shared in their humanity so that by his death he might destroy him who holds the power of death—that is, the devil—and free those who all their lives were held in slavery by their fear of death."

When we put those texts together we see a great pattern. We see that Jesus endured a human birth to give us a new spiritual birth. He occupied a stable that we might occupy a mansion. He had an earthly mother so that we might have a heavenly Father. He became subject that we might be free. He left His glory to give us glory. He was poor that we might be rich. He was welcomed by shepherds at His birth whereas we at our birth are welcomed by angels. He was hunted by Herod that we might be delivered from the grasp of Satan. That is the great paradox of the Christmas story. It is that which makes it irresistibly attractive. It is the reversal of roles at God's cost for our benefit.

THREE LESSONS

Should it not be for the benefit of countless others also? It will be if we understand the paradox and then live it out in our lives.

First, no Christian should judge by appearances, especially by those that impress the world greatly. We tend to think more of a person who has an important position in this world—if he is a prominent professional person, perhaps a doctor or a lawyer, or if he is famous. James noted in his day how the chief places at feasts were given to those who had position or fine clothing. But he rebuked those actions, saying, "Have you not discriminated among yourselves and become judges with evil thoughts? Listen, my dear brothers: Has not God chosen those who are poor in the eyes of the world to be rich in faith and to inherit the kingdom he promised to those who love him?" (James 2:4–5). If the birth of Christ is to teach anything, it is to teach that God can choose to hide the greatest of gifts in the poorest of packages. He wrapped His own Son in a manger.

Second, we should learn that it is impossible for us to judge the end of anything by its beginning. The end of this story, the story of the birth of Jesus, is found in those great passages in Revelation in which the whole creation is brought forth to praise God. There the four and twenty elders fall down on their faces before the Lamb and sing a new song, saying:

> You are worthy to take the scroll
>   and to open its seals,
> because you were slain,
>   and with your blood you purchased men for God
>   from every tribe and language and people and
>   nation. (Revelation 5:9)

The angels sing:

> Worthy is the Lamb, who was slain,
> to receive power and wealth and wisdom and strength
> and honor and glory and praise! (v. 12)

After these, every living creature worships Jesus, saying:

> To him who sits on the throne and to the Lamb
> be praise and honor and glory and power,
>   for ever and ever! (v. 13)

Surely there is no more exalted position, no more brilliant success, in all the universe or all world history. Yet who would have imagined this outcome from the lowly beginning in Bethlehem so many centuries ago?

Do not be disheartened by what are apparently your own small efforts to spread the gospel or by your own weak beginnings in the Christian life. God is not finished with you yet. His gospel has not yet run its course. He has told us that we will be like Jesus one day. He has promised that His Word will not return to Him void. Take heart! You cannot see the end of these things from the beginning.

LOVE STOOPS TO CONQUER

Finally, there is a lesson in what the Christian life should be. The message of the incarnation is that we should humble ourselves and give of ourselves for others. At Christmas we sometimes get quite sentimental and even maudlin about this theme. We note that Jesus was rejected by people even at His birth, and we like to think that we are not like them. We sing, "Oh, come to my heart, Lord Jesus; there is room in my heart for thee." But often that is no more than empty sentiment. If it were more, we would have room in our hearts not only for Jesus but for others also.

Jesus emptied Himself for us. He laid aside His great glory in order to help us. Do we lay aside our prerogatives to help those who need help? We should be willing and should actually help others at any season of the year, but at Christmas think especially of those who are left out of the joy that belongs to most of us. We have our families, our parties, our other good times. But our communities are literally filled with others who will not be a part of these things and so feel the loneliness of Christmas deeply.

"Loneliness?" you ask. "At Christmas?" Yes, particularly at Christmas! For thousands, this is the worst time of the year. For, while others are enjoying the family times, the lonely are left to themselves and to sad memories. For some it will be the first Christmas since the death of a beloved husband or wife, son or daughter. They will be reminded of their loss with every carol, every smile, every "Merry Christmas!" Others have poor health, and they will be left out. Still others are separated from their families—foreign students in our country, those who have to work through the holidays, spouses who are divorced from their children (as well as the former husband or wife) through the failure of their marriage. All these are left out.

Can you not include one or two in your Christmas—some student, some nurse, some single person, some poor derelict, someone who can never return the favor of a family Christmas to you?

Do you say, "Oh, but Christmas is a family time, and I don't want to spoil it by including someone else."

If those are your thoughts, remember that you were on the outside once. You were separated from Christmas in two ways. First, you were likely a Gentile, and Christ was Israel's Messiah. Second, you were a sinner, and you were barred from God's blessings by sin. Jesus came to include you. He came to die for you so that you, who were unclean and unholy, might be cleansed of sin and made holy. If you know Him and love Him, you will reach out to others.

8

No Room
IN THE Inn

A NUMBER OF YEARS AGO a well-known Bible teacher was invited to take part in a Christmas television program. It was to be a panel discussion, and the theme was to be "The Coming of Jesus Two Thousand Years Ago." When the time for the program had come and the participants were assembled, the moderator of the program began the discussion by remarking how beautiful the Christmas story is and how eagerly the world waited for the coming of the infant Christ in Bethlehem so long ago.

A number of comments were made. Then the Bible teacher had his turn to speak. He returned to the moderator's opening comment and said that at the risk of sounding contradictory it was necessary for him to say that the remarks just made were far from being accurate. "The world did not wait eagerly for the Christ child," he said. "On the contrary, the world was so busy with its affairs that it would not even make room for Him to be born. He had to be born in a stable. Besides, no one would even have noticed the birth if God had not sent angels to announce it to shepherds and sent a star to guide the eastern kings to Palestine." He then pointed out that it is precisely the same today. "Men and women express sentimental thoughts about the infant Jesus as they go about their own affairs and pleasures at Christmastime. But few pay any attention to the real Christ, and they do not make room for Him in their lives."

What the Bible teacher said on that occasion was true; and it is as true for us as for any earlier generation, perhaps even more so. We are certainly busy, and few, so far as we can tell, have room for Jesus. The Christmas story describes it: "She [Mary] gave birth to her firstborn, a son. She wrapped him in cloths and placed him in a manger, because there was no room for them in the inn" (Luke 2:7).

No Room Anywhere

Of course, there were other places besides the inn that had no room for Him. Indeed, the fact that there was no room in the inn teaches us that in truth there was no room for Him anywhere.

There was no room for Him in the palaces of this world's kings. Caesar would not make room. The idea of the great

Augustus making room for the humble carpenter from Nazareth and his pregnant companion Mary is preposterous. Nor
would Herod make room. Herod ruled within a dozen miles
of where Christ should be born; but so far was he from making
room that he actually plotted to have the young child killed
when the birth was at last made known to him by the wise
men. Today is no different. On this point the great Baptist
preacher, Charles Haddon Spurgeon, once wrote:

> Alas! my brethren, seldom is there room for Christ in pal-
> aces! How could the kings of earth receive the Lord? He
> is the Prince of Peace, and they delight in war! He breaks
> their bows and cuts their spears in sunder; he burneth their
> war-chariots in the fire. How could kings accept the humble
> Savior? They love grandeur and pomp, and he is all simplicity
> and meekness. He is a carpenter's son, and the fisherman's
> companion. How can princes find room for the new-born
> monarch? Why he teaches us to do to others as we would
> that they should do to us, and this is a thing which kings
> would find very hard to reconcile with the knavish tricks of
> politics and the grasping designs of ambition. O great ones
> of earth, I am but little astonished that amid your glories,
> and pleasures, and wars, and councils, ye forget the Anointed,
> and cast out the Lord of All.[1]

Notice too that there was no room for Christ in the courts
of the philosophers. At the beginning, the coming of Christ
was unknown to such men, but when it was made known they
laughed at the gospel.

---

1. Charles Haddon Spurgeon, "No Room for Christ in the Inn," *Metropolitan Tab-
ernacle Pulpit* (1969), 8:702.

"Surely this could not have been true in Israel," we say. "In Israel the leaders of the people knew the prophets and could even tell where the Christ should be born." But we remember that Herod inquired of those very men where the Christ should be born; and, though they could answer correctly and though they knew of the wise men's visit, not one ventured to Bethlehem to greet the infant Christ and worship Him.

How seldom do we find a regard for Christ in the seats of learning? How few of the wise, how few of this world's professors, how few of the most learned of religious leaders have room for Jesus!

"But surely these were not all the important people that we might consider," someone argues. "Were there not good families who might have taken Him in?" Undoubtedly there were good families in Bethlehem, but I do not read that these good families made room for the woman in labor or later welcomed her child. They may have been very gracious to each other. On occasion they may even have done charitable deeds for the poor. But there was no more room for Jesus among those excellent, well-to-do families than there was in the palaces of the kings or in the courts of the philosophers.

REJECTED OF MEN

I can imagine that at this point we may be experiencing some little surges of self-satisfaction. "For," we argue, "though it is true that there was no place for Christ among the wise, mighty, or noble of this world, surely there was a place for Him among the common people, such as ourselves. We would welcome Him." But would we? We must remember that in Christ's day inns were not the stopping places of the rich or noble. The rich stayed with their friends. Inns were the stopping places of the common folks, who had nowhere else to go. It was precisely the inn that had no place for Jesus.

We sometimes amuse ourselves by thinking that common people are more charitable or sympathetic than the rich. We speculate that they are more susceptible to the claims of religion. But it is not so. Rather, the Bible teaches us,

> We *all*, like sheep, have gone astray,
>> *each of us* has turned to his own way;
> and the Lord has laid on him
>> the iniquity of us all.
>> (Isaiah 53:6, emphasis added)

It is easy to understand why the common folk who filled the inn on that first Christmas did not receive Him. For one thing, others had simply come first. The inn was full, and why should one who had possessed the wisdom to arrive early make way for those who came late, regardless of how pressing the need was? For another thing, there was obvious indifference. True, the woman was with child. But so were thousands of other women. Perhaps if they had possessed money, they might have been welcomed. But they did not. They were poor. So there was literally no incentive to show concern or attention, and Christ was crowded out.

Am I describing your life? One commentator writes, "Every chamber of the soul is so filled with human interests that there is little room for Christ. There is little vital interest in him. There is little, if any, time for him. And this is so, simply because our time is demanded by a thousand other things, our interest is drawn off in a thousand other directions, and our life is crowded to the full with possessions and pleasures until, strange though it seems, there is no room for the Savior except in the stable."[2]

I wonder if Jesus is in the stable of your life, or whether He is at its core. Until He has entered the door and reigns upon the throne of your life, you cannot regard yourself as being in any better position than those who slept comfortably while Mary gave birth to her child in a stable.

DO YOU HAVE ROOM?

Do *you* have room for Jesus? Do you have *room* for Christ? "I have room for Christ, but I am unworthy," says someone. Of course, you are unworthy! This world is unworthy of Christ, its Creator and King. But still He came to it; and, as if to make the truth plain beyond all question, He had His birth with sheep and donkeys.

"My life is so vile," says another. But wasn't the stable vile? Did it not also smell of corruption?

"But I am afraid of Him," says a third. What? Afraid of Jesus? What harm has He done? To which of us has He not done good?

Bible teacher Harry Ironside told the story of an old woman who was in distress because of her deep poverty. She was living

2. James Hastings and Edward Hastings, eds., *The Speaker's Bible* (Grand Rapids: Baker, 1971), 9:93.

in a little garret in London and was afraid that one day the police would come and arrest her because of her debts. It happened that a good Christian minister heard of her plight and raised money to pay off her creditors. Then, with the receipt for the debt in his pocket and with provision for her present needs, he went to find her. The neighbors knew her only by the name "Old Betty." So when he got to the building where she lived, the minister asked, "Can you tell me where Old Betty lives?"

He was told to go up the stairs to a certain room. He went to the door and knocked. He waited, but there was no answer. He knocked again. No answer! He called, "Old Betty, are you in there?" Nothing!

At last he went back down the stairs and started to leave. But as he left, her neighbors asked him, "Did you find her?"

"No," he answered. "She is not in."

"Oh, she's in, all right. She's just not letting you in. She's afraid you are one of her creditors, and she is just not opening the door."

When he heard this the minister went back up the stairs to the room and called out, "Old Betty, let me in! I'm the minister, and I've come to see you."

"Oh," came a voice from within. "I thought you were the police, and I was afraid to open the door." When the door finally opened, the minister told her that friends had raised money to cancel her debt, had paid it, and had sent him to tell her that, give her the receipt, and present her with an additional amount for her current needs. Old Betty was overwhelmed and embarrassed. "Just think," she said, "I locked and bolted the door against you. I was afraid to let you in."[3]

3. H. A. Ironside, *Illustrations of Bible Truth* (Chicago: Moody, 1945), pp. 65–67.

You and I are Old Betty. The minister is Christ. We have been afraid to open to Him. Yet He has undertaken to cancel the debt of our sin by His own death, and He has come to provide for us now. He is our best friend, but we have kept Him out. Many will admit that this has been true of them until by the sweet compulsion of His grace the Lord Jesus Christ moved them to open the door and admit Him into the deep recesses of their lives. These will testify that they did not make a mistake in yielding to Him. They will say that was the best decision they ever made. Have you opened the door? Have you made room for the Savior?

If not, let Him be born in your soul today. Do not say, "I hope that I will have room for Him." Make room for Him! The Bible says, "Today, if you hear his voice, do not harden your hearts as you did in the rebellion" (Hebrews 3:7–8). The Bible says, "Now is the time of God's favor, now is the day of salvation" (2 Corinthians 6:2).

No Room for You

My fourth point is a warning: If you make room for Christ, then from this day on, the world will have no room for you. We see this in Luke 2:7. For, notice, it does not say "because there was no room for *him* in the inn." It says "for *them*." That includes Mary and Joseph as well as the infant Jesus.

Who are Christ's mother and father and sister and brother today? Are they not those who do the will of Christ's Father, as He said (Matthew 12:48–50)? Are they not those who open their hearts to Him and follow Him? Well, then, if you have followed Him, the world will have no more room for you than it had for Him. You must not think that if you follow Jesus you will be praised for doing so. The angels will rejoice over every sinner who repents, no matter how insignificant in the world's eyes. But the world will not rejoice. The world will scorn your decision. The world will seek to put you down. Then, if it cannot succeed in getting you to renounce your decision or compromise your stand, it will turn its back on you and go its own way, shutting you out.

That is what Jesus foretold. It was He who said, "If you belonged to the world, it would love you as its own. As it is, you do not belong to the world, but I have chosen you out of the world. That is why the world hates you" (John 15:19). Jesus said, "Woe to you when all men speak well of you" (Luke 6:26). Jesus said to His disciples, "In this world you will have trouble. But take heart! I have overcome the world" (John 16:33). To be Christ's follower is to be a person without a country, a displaced person. It is to follow Him into the poverty of the early years at Nazareth, the loneliness of the itinerant ministry, eventually to the cross, all the time knowing that the disciple, like the Master, has no place to lay his head.

MANY ROOMS

But though the world will have no room for you from the day that you decide to follow Jesus, *He* will have room. He has gone to prepare the most glorious rooms for each of His followers. He said, "Do not let your hearts be troubled. Trust in God; trust also in me. In my Father's house are many rooms; if it were not so, I would have told you. I am going there to prepare a place for you. And if I go and prepare a place for you, I will come back and take you to be with me that you also may be where I am" (John 14:1–3).

Are you ready to serve Christ on such terms? Will you serve Him when there is no room below, only a cross, yet knowing that He who went to a cross has also gone on to prepare a place for you in heaven? Others have followed Him and have rejoiced in the grace that has given them such an opportunity.

9

The Men Who Missed Christmas

IN THE FIRST WEEK of June 1944, the German general Rommel was strengthening the fortifications of the beaches of western France against the imminent Allied invasion of Hitler's Europe. This was the Rommel who had gained fame as a military strategist in North Africa, and he was convinced that in this stage of the war, if the Allies should ever gain a foothold in France, the war would be lost for Germany. He had done much to put the defenses in readiness, but as the first week of June drew to an end and the weather off the Atlantic coast grew worse, Rommel felt he could spare a few days away from the feverish action. His wife's birthday was June 6, and he had a birthday present for her. Consequently, he left the front on the fifth of June and was in Berlin with his family when the Allied invasion came the next day.

Here was a man who had sensed the importance of the greatest single military invasion in history. He had prepared for it. But when it came, he was busy with other things and missed his opportunity. Actually, as we know, in the confusion of that important day the combined British and American forces gained their toehold on the coast of Normandy and were then able to push on toward the Rhine and the eventual destruction of the Third Reich.

Many persons throughout history have had Rommel's experience. But of all those experiences perhaps none has been more tragic than that of the men who missed Christmas. When I speak of the men who missed Christmas I am speaking, naturally, of the men who missed the first Christmas, who missed the birth of the Lord Jesus Christ. Yet, in another sense, I am also speaking of many who miss Christmas today. These miss the most important thing in life, and yet—here is the tragedy—there is no good reason why they should miss it.

THE INNKEEPER

The first of the men who missed Christmas was quite obviously the innkeeper. The Bible does not mention the man explicitly. Probably by the time the story of the birth of Jesus Christ was put into writing no one remembered who he was. There was no reason to remember him. Still, there certainly was an innkeeper, for when the Bible tells us that Mary "gave birth to her firstborn, a son, [and] wrapped him in cloths and placed him in a manger, because there was no room for them in the inn" (Luke 2:7), the verse implies the existence of this man. In the hustle and bustle of the season the innkeeper missed the most important birth in history.

He should not have missed it, of course, simply because he was so close to it. The decree of the emperor Augustus brought the family of Jesus to *his* town, Bethlehem. Mary and Joseph stood on his doorstep, perhaps even entered his waiting room, stood before his desk. The child was born in his stable, almost under his nose. And yet his preoccupation with his business kept him from it.

Let me share this dramatized account of the innkeeper's reasoning. It comes from a recent book by the distinguished American writer Frederick Buechner.

"I speak to you as men of the world," said the Innkeeper. "Not as idealists but as realists. Do you know what it is like to run an inn—to run a business, a family, to run anything in this world for that matter, even your own life: It is like being lost in a forest of a million trees," said the Innkeeper, "and each tree is a thing to be done. Is there fresh linen on all the beds? Did the children put on their coats before they went out? Has the letter been written, the book read? Is there money enough left in the bank? Today we have food in our bellies and clothes on our backs, but what can we do to make sure we will have them still tomorrow? A million trees. A million things. . . . Finally we have eyes for nothing else, and whatever we see turns into a thing."[1]

1. Frederick Buechner, *The Magnificent Defeat* (New York: Seabury, 1966), pp. 66–67.

Am I pressing the point too much to say that the world is filled with innkeepers today, materialistic people who miss the meaning of Christmas simply because their business, parties, Christmas cards, trees, or tinsel seem too pressing? If that were not the case, there would not be so many grim faces in our stores or so many exhausted, sleepy people in our churches the Sunday before Christmas.

Do not think that I am merely speaking to non-Christians at this point. I am probably not speaking to them much at all. Who would berate Caesar Augustus for having missed Christmas? He was too far away. There was no possibility of his having found it. We would not berate the Greeks or countless others. Actually I am speaking to Christians, for they are the ones who should take note of the birth of Christ deeply and yet often do not do it.

A number of years ago a minister named A. W. Tozer was very concerned about the feverish materialism of today's Christians. He wrote:

Every age has its own characteristics. Right now we are in an age of religious complexity. The simplicity which is in Christ is rarely found among us. In its stead are programs, methods, organizations and a world of nervous activities which occupy time and attention but can never satisfy the longing of the heart. The shallowness of our inner experience, the hollowness of our worship, and that servile imitation of the world which marks our promotional methods all testify that we, in this day, know God only imperfectly, and the peace of God scarcely at all. If we would find God amid all the religious externals we must first determine to find him, and then proceed in the way of simplicity. Now as always God discovers himself to "babes" and hides himself in thick darkness from the wise and the prudent. We must simplify our approach to him.[2]

HEROD

The second man who missed Christmas was Herod. Herod was the king of Judea or, as we should more accurately say, an under-king of a border province of the far-flung Roman Empire. There was nothing likeable about Herod. He was a sly old fox, guilty of many murders, including at least one wife and three sons. He probably had no religion. He was a cynic. He knew the traditions of Israel, but he only half-believed them, if he believed them at all. Yet he should have found Christmas, if only because he had a large stake in the outcome.

Matthew is the one who tells Herod's story. Herod was at home in Jerusalem when news reached him that wise men had come from the East. They were asking where they could find the king of the Jews, the one born recently. Herod did not have anyone like that in his palace. There were no recent births. Besides, he was aware that the wise men were talking about the Messiah, and he knew of no Messiah. Talk like that was dangerous. Herod therefore called the religious leaders to find out where the future king should be born. The answer was "Bethlehem!" After that he called the wise men and persuaded them to report to him if their search in Bethlehem proved fruitful.

2. A. W. Tozer, *The Pursuit of God* (Harrisburg, Pa.: Christian Publications, 1948), pp. 17–18.

"Go and make a careful search for the child. As soon as you find him, report to me, so that I too may go and worship him" (Matthew 2:8). It was a sly maneuver, for murder, not worship, was in the old king's heart. It was a pity also, for Herod knew of the birth. He even knew its significance. Yet he missed it through the encrusted habit of greed and self-interest.

Does that describe you? I do not mean the question to be insulting, but isn't it true that many people miss practically everything good in life through self-interest? If that is true of such things as friendship, beauty, love, good times, and happiness, how much truer is it that many miss Jesus? If you are like Herod, even in a small way, perhaps you should pay attention to something Jesus said: "What good is it for a man to gain the whole world, yet forfeit his soul?" (Mark 8:36). Your real self-interest lies in finding the one who loved you and died to be your Savior.

The Religious Leaders

There were others who also missed Christmas. Those were the religious leaders, the chief priests, and the scribes. They of all men should not have missed the birth of Christ, for they had the Scriptures. They were the ones who could tell Herod where the Christ was to be born. They knew it was to be Bethlehem. Yet they did not leave their own homes or the palace to investigate His arrival.

What was it that kept their leaders from going along with the wise men? We do not know for certain, of course. But it may well have been their pride in the fact that Herod had called them instead of others and that they had been able to produce the right answer to his question.

We see that in the religious world. There are sectors of the church of Jesus Christ in which almost any Bible question will receive a right answer. Yet in many of those places there is no real hunger after God, and thus the vital, joyous, and rewarding reality of the presence of the Lord Jesus Christ is lacking. Do not misunderstand. Accurate Bible knowledge is important. It is only through a knowledge of the Scriptures that we can know Jesus. It is only through knowing Jesus that we can know God. We must study our Bibles. I spend most of my own life studying and teaching the Bible. Yet knowing the content of the Bible is not enough. If we are to be all that God intends us to be, we must see beyond the Book—through it, if you will—to its author.

Do you know the author? If you do, it will make a difference in your life. It will satisfy you. It will make you forget yourself. Above all, it will teach you to love as God loved us when He gave us Jesus.

Francis Schaeffer has written:

As Christians we must not minimize the need to give honest answers to honest questions. We should have an intellectual apologetic. The Bible commands it and Christ and Paul exemplify it. In the synagogue, in the marketplace, in homes and in almost every conceivable kind of situation, Jesus and Paul discussed Christianity. It is likewise the Christian's task to be able to give an honest answer to an honest question and then to give it.

Yet, without true Christians loving one another, Christ says the world cannot be expected to listen, even when we give proper answers. Let us be careful, indeed, to spend a lifetime studying to give honest answers. For years the orthodox, evangelical church has done this very poorly. So it is well to spend time learning to answer the questions of men who are about us. But after we have done our best to communicate to a lost world, still we must never forget that the final apologetic which Jesus gives is the observable love of true Christians.[3]

THOSE WHO FOUND IT

It would be entirely wrong not to point out that although there were many who did not find Christmas—millions, in fact—there were nevertheless some who did find it. They were not the kings of this world. They were not the religious leaders. They were not the thousands who were engrossed in the countless minutia of materialistic lives. They were just poor folk who were looking to God and to whom God came.

We can think of several of them. There were the shepherds. They were nobody in the social structure of the ancient East. Most people thought poorly of them. They were not able to testify in a court of law, for their testimony was considered unreliable. Yet they saw the angels. The wise men also found Christmas. They were not even Jews—everybody knew that God's promised salvation was of the Jews. Yet the wise men saw the star. Finally, there were those like Simeon and Anna, poor but saintly folks, who, like many others, "were looking forward to the redemption of Jerusalem" (Luke 2:38). No one would have given a second thought to those poor folk. They were not important. Yet they saw and even held God's treasure.

3. Francis Schaeffer, *The Church at the End of the Twentieth Century* (Downers Grove, Ill.: Inter-Varsity, 1970), pp. 139–40.

Why did these people find Christmas? I think there are two answers. The first is that they were *honest enough* to admit their need. The self-sufficient would never have made the trip to the manger; they do not do it today. But that does not describe the ones who find Christ. These people know they need a Savior. Second, they were *humble enough* to receive the Lord Jesus Christ when He came. No doubt there were levels of comprehension. Perhaps the shepherds or the wise men or even Simeon or Anna did not understand much. But whatever they understood they received, for we are told in each case that they praised God for the birth of the Lord.

In Europe everyone who attends a university gets the same basic training in the classics and the basic tools of religion, so that whether he becomes a doctor, lawyer, chemist, or a professor, he is only a few steps away from being fully qualified for the ministry. In one European city a German pastor was called away from his little parish in an emergency and, since there was no time for him to get another preacher to fill his pulpit the following Sunday, he called upon the tutor of a noble family who lived in the neighborhood.

The man was not a Christian. When the pastor called upon him to preach, he replied, "How can I preach what I do not believe?"

"What?" said the pastor in astonishment. "You believe in God, don't you?"

"Yes," replied the tutor, "I believe in God."

"And do you not believe that we should love Him?" asked the pastor.

"Yes," said the tutor again, "I believe that we should."

"Well," replied the pastor, "I will give you a text to preach on. It is in the words of Jesus: 'Love the Lord your God with all your heart and with all your soul and with all your mind' [Matthew 22:37]."

The tutor agreed to the text. So the pastor went to keep his appointment, and the tutor sat down to study the text and write out an outline for his message. He was a skeptic, you understand, a rationalist. So he very rationally wrote out his first point and gave a reason for it. The first point was: "We must love God." Second, he wrote: "We must love Him with all our powers; indeed, nothing less could satisfy Him." Third, he wrote: "Do we thus love Him?" His conscience then forced him to put down, "No, we do not."

Later, this man wrote about his experience. He said, "Without any previously formed plan, I was brought to add to my notes, 'We need a Savior.'" Here light broke in upon his darkened soul. He said, "I understood that I had not loved God, that I did need a Savior, that Jesus Christ was that Savior; and then I loved Him and I clung to Him at once. On the morrow I preached the sermon, and the third point was the chief—the need of Jesus and the necessity of trusting such a Savior."

The wise men, whether they are shepherds or magi, are those who acknowledge their need and humble themselves to receive the Savior. Only those find Christmas.

10

The Men Who Found Christmas

ONE TRAGEDY of the first Christmas is that so many came close to Christmas yet missed it all. We have looked at some of their stories. There were the political leaders of the time: Caesar Augustus and Quirinius, the governor of Syria. Those men possessed everything the world has to offer, yet they missed God's greatest gift. The innkeeper also missed Christmas. He was closest to it, but he probably was kept from Christmas by the pressure of business and by a preoccupation with things. Herod missed the birth of Jesus. His failure was most blame-worthy, because he had been told of the birth by the wise men yet missed it through hatred of the one he supposed to be a pretender to the throne. Herod wanted to kill the child but was deceived by the wise men, who had been instructed by God to return to their own country by another route. Last of all, the religious leaders missed Christmas. They missed it even though they had been told of the birth and even knew the Scripture passage in Micah which told where the Messiah should be born.

But that is only half the story. It is true that the political and religious leaders and the others missed Christmas. But they are not the only people in the narrative. The shepherds to whom the angels appeared while they were tending their sheep in the fields around Bethlehem found Christmas. And the wise men who saw the Messiah's star came to worship Him. The wise men and shepherds have become models for those who find Christmas in any era.

A MAGNIFICENT CONTRAST

It is hard to imagine a greater contrast than the one between those two groups of people who found Christmas. An obvious contrast is between that which was low and that which was high on the social scale of the time. The shepherds were low. They were looked down upon as being among the basest elements of society. They were despised and mistrusted. They were thought to be crafty and dishonest, and their ability to make off with things that did not belong to them was proverbial. So bad was their reputation that they were not even allowed to bear testimony in a court of law. It was assumed that such people would lie. In most people's minds shepherds were like gypsies, vagrants, and con men all rolled into one.

What about the wise men? Quite obviously they were at the other end of the scale. They were men of influence. We notice that when they came to Jerusalem, looking for the one who had been born king of the Jews, they had no trouble gaining admission to Herod's palace or even obtaining an audience with the king himself. The shepherds would not even have been allowed in the outer courtyard.

A second contrast concerns the financial status of the two groups of people. It is between the poorest of the poor and the richest of the rich. The shepherds had nothing. Oh, they had their work, and that was better than being beggars, as some others were. But as far as work was concerned, nothing paid less. A manual laborer did much better than those who were entrusted with sheep. When the shepherds came to Bethlehem to see what had come to pass, they quickly went to "spread the word" concerning the child (Luke 2:17); but they did not give gifts. They had none to offer. On the other hand, the wise men were obviously men of substance. They had money enough to take a long journey from the East to Jerusalem, as well as having the leisure to do it. Moreover, when they arrived they presented the child and His family with gifts of gold, incense, and myrrh.

Education is another point of wide contrast. Shepherds were among the "people of the land," which meant that they were not even educated enough to read the Jewish Scriptures. They had no formal education whatever. By contrast, the magi were famed for their knowledge. We do not know precisely who those particular wise men were or where they came from. But, in general, wise men were noted for their knowledge of religious documents, "magic" or healing arts, astrology, and astronomy. They were the professors of the day. When the Messiah's star appeared, they were the ones who saw it and discerned its meaning.

Finally, there is a contrast between the proximity of the shepherds to Bethlehem, where Jesus was born, and the fact that the wise men came from a great distance. We do not know exactly how far the wise men traveled, since "from the east" is a very general description. But since Herod inquired of them exactly when the star had appeared and then later killed all the male children of Bethlehem from the age of two years down, it is probably that the star had appeared between one and two years before that time and that the wise men had been on their journey for many long months. They came from the far reaches of the world, whereas the shepherds were as close to the birth as the hills around Bethlehem.

I do not know how the story could say more clearly that Christ is for anyone who will have Him and that Christ is for you, whoever you may be. You may be unimportant in the eyes of most people or you may be very important, a mere cog in the machine or a celebrity. You may be poor or rich. You may be ignorant or well educated. You may be near Christ or far from Him. None of those things matters, for the simple reason that Jesus did not come to be the Savior of the rich or poor only, or the wise or foolish only, or anything else. He came to be the Savior of the *world*, and that includes you. That is the great news of Christmas!

A COMMON EXPERIENCE

The shepherds and wise men were as different as they could possibly be. Yet in all the important things their experience was similar, and that set them off from those who missed Christmas far more than their differences set them off from each other. Their experiences contained four great similarities.

First, the shepherds and the wise men each received an announcement of Christ's birth. That was most spectacular in the case of the shepherds, for "the glory of the Lord shone around them" and an angel said to them, "Do not be afraid. I bring you good news of great joy that will be for all the people. Today in the town of David a Savior has been born to you; he is Christ the Lord. This will be a sign to you: You will find a baby wrapped in cloths and lying in a manger" (Luke 2:9–12). The announcement was then expanded by the addition of a great company of angels who praised God, saying, "Glory to God in the highest, and on earth peace to men on whom his favor rests" (vv. 13–14). This was both visual and verbal. It was a magnificent thing.

But was the announcement to the magi less magnificent from their perspective? We do not know for certain what the star of Bethlehem was. It has been explained as a comet, a special configuration or overlapping of planets, even the appearance of God's Shekinah glory—which may be the best explanation of all since the "star" guided the wise men and eventually brought them to the very house where Christ was. Whatever the case, the star was the kind of thing the wise men dealt with and was therefore well suited as the vehicle of their particular revelation.

Those two revelations—one to the shepherds and the other to the wise men—were magnificent, among other reasons, because they were the first new word from God in what had proved to be a long time of silence. In biblical studies, the centuries between Malachi, the last book of the Old Testament, and the coming of Christ are referred to as "the silent years" because there was no new word from God in that period. Malachi wrote about four hundred years before Christ. So for four hundred years the people of God had lived without any sign from God and without any prophet to speak the words of God to them. They were waiting for the Messiah. Then suddenly the silence was broken. The sky was filled with angels, and the message of joy was proclaimed to all peoples: "Today in the town of David a Savior has been born to you; he is Christ the Lord."

Our experience parallels that of the wise men and shepherds at this point, but is actually superior to theirs. The shepherds received a vision of the glory of God, accompanied by angels. The wise men saw a star. But we have received the Scriptures, which are the very Word of God and are described to us as "a light shining in a dark place" (2 Peter 1:19). The context of that reference is interesting. It comes from the second letter of Peter and follows a section in which Peter has cited the fact that he was an eyewitness of the heavenly glory of Jesus Christ. He was one of those who was with Jesus on the mountain when He was transformed and a voice from God was heard, saying, "This is my Son, whom I love; with him I am well pleased" (2 Peter 1:17). That experience of Peter (and of James and John, who were with him) would compare quite favorably with the experience of the shepherds in the fields of Bethlehem or that of the magi as they studied the heavens. Yet immediately after that Peter speaks of the Scripture as being even "more certain" and concludes: "You will do well to pay attention to it, as to a light shining in a dark place, until the day dawns and the morning star rises in your hearts" (v. 19). In spite of his experience, Peter valued the written Word of God above everything.

Second, the shepherds and the wise men each obeyed God's summons. In the film *Close Encounters of the Third Kind*, a number of people received invitations by an extraterrestrial people to a visit they were soon going to make to earth. The plot of the movie was in the heroic efforts of these people to get to the meeting place and be there when the spaceship came down.

That was the kind of invitation the shepherds and wise men received. Only theirs was to a far more significant encounter. This visit to earth was not merely a visit of an alien people but of the very God of the universe Himself. It was an invitation to the birth of Jesus, God's unique Son.

Can we imagine the shepherds or wise men refusing that unprecedented invitation? Perhaps. The magi lived at a great distance from Jerusalem and were alerted to the child's birth only by the appearance of His star. They might have reasoned: "The star probably announces the birth of a Savior-King in Judea, but of course we could be mistaken. The way to Jerusalem is long. Others will probably be paying their respects. We don't need to go. It would be a lot more convenient if we could stay here." The shepherds, too, might have refused the invitation. They might have said: "We are not dressed for the occasion. We have nothing to bring. We are not fit company for Him who is announced by angels." They might even have asked, "But who will care for our sheep? Who will tend to the things for which we are responsible?" Neither the wise men nor shepherds did that. Instead of making excuses the shepherds said, "Let's go to Bethlehem and see this thing that has happened, which the Lord has told us about" (Luke 2:15).

I wonder if you have been as obedient to God as those shepherds, who were so low on the social scale of their day, or the wise men, who were so removed from the happenings in Judea. You know the story of Christmas. You even know the gospel of Jesus' death for sinners, for which Christmas was but a preparation. You know the invitation of Christ: "Come to me, all you who are weary and burdened, and I will give you rest" (Matthew 11:28). Have you responded to that invitation? Have you obeyed God's summons? You have not found Christmas, nor will you ever find it, until you do.

That leads to the third step in the shepherds' and wise men's common experience. After they had each received the announcement and obeyed God's summons by going to Bethlehem, they found the Savior. That was the climax of their experience and the peak moment of their stories. They found that the words of the angel and the message of the star were not misleading. They discovered that God's communications were not lies. God's Son had been born. The Savior had come. He was there for all who would leave what they were doing and come to Him.

That is no less true today. In our day people talk as if it were hard to find Christ, or, to put it in other language, they act as if it were hard to find their way through the superstitions of religion to the truth about God. What gross misunderstanding! To talk like that is to suggest that God is lost and that it is up to us to find Him. He is not lost nor is the truth lost. We are the ones who are lost, and the difficulties are in us and not in either God or His gospel.

Do not say that the truth cannot be found. Jesus said, "I am . . . the truth" (John 14:6). Jesus is presented in Scripture. If you would find Him, you must search the Scriptures. As you do, pray like this: "God, I am not certain what the truth is concerning religious things. But I believe that if You exist and if Jesus Christ is truly Your Son and the Savior You have sent into the world, then You should be able to show this to me as I study the Bible. If Jesus is the Savior, I want to find Him. If I do find Him, I promise to be His disciple and serve Him all my days."

A man once came to Bible teacher Reuben A. Torrey complaining that he had investigated Christianity but had concluded that there was nothing to it. It was all a sham. Torrey challenged him to read John's gospel and to pray along the lines I have just suggested. The man agreed to do what was asked, but he was convinced that there was still nothing to Christianity. They met two weeks later, and Torrey asked how the man's spiritual journey was coming.

"You know, there was something to that," he said. "Ever since I have done what you suggested I feel as if I have been caught up and am being carried along by the Niagara River. The first thing you know I shall become a shouting Methodist."

Several more weeks went by, and when the two met again, the man had become a Christian. He testified: "I can't understand now how I ever listened to anything else."[1] If you are not yet a Christian, this can become your story if you only

---

1. Reuben A. Torrey, *The Bible and Its Christ* (New York: Revell, 1904), pp. 53–57.

turn to the account of Jesus' birth, life, death, and resurrection with an honest mind.

The story of the experience of the shepherds and wise men did not stop with their discovery. Thus far they had: (1) received an announcement, (2) obeyed God's summons, and (3) found the Savior. But now, having found the Savior, they did a fourth thing in a common response to their discovery: they worshiped. That is stated clearly in the case of the wise men. "On coming to the house, they saw the child with his mother Mary, and they bowed down and worshiped him" (Matthew 2:11). We are told only that the shepherds worshiped God (Luke 2:20), but we are no doubt to assume that they had first worshiped the child as the Son of God. We remember that the angels had identified Him as "the Lord" (v. 11).

A ROMANIAN CHRISTMAS

There will always be worship when a person finds the true meaning of Christmas, which is to say, when he or she finds Christ to be the Savior. That is how we know the person has found Him, and that worship will always take place regardless of any outward opposition.

Some years ago I had the opportunity of getting to know the Reverend Joseph Ton, a Baptist pastor from Romania. He is now in the United States, having been expelled from his homeland by Communists because of his stand for the gospel. Recently he wrote of the traditional Romanian Christmas in which, before the Communists took over, every village prepared its own somewhat unique celebration. Each family would slaughter a pig, which would be the staple of the traditional Christmas feast. Everyone would carol. Ton described how children would begin their caroling early in the morning of the day before Christmas. They would go from door to door with cloth bags on their backs, singing and collecting nuts, apples, and cakes, much as children in America collect candy at Halloween. Toward evening the teenage boys would carol. They were organized in bigger groups and would put on shows depicting various stories or legends. Later at night the older people would start moving about from house to house. Old hatreds would be set aside, and on Christmas Day everybody would be in church together.

Then came Communism. Christmas was no longer a legal holiday. Everybody had to go to work on that day, as on any other day. For many people the old traditions ceased. But among the truly born-again people the traditions concerned with worshiping Christ and celebrating His birth did not perish. Today in Romania every evangelical church has services in the morning and evening (before and after work), not only on Christmas Day but on the twenty-sixth of December as well, called the "second day of Christmas." And the caroling goes on!

Ton testifies that for many years the police worked hard to stop people from caroling. One year in one of the towns the local police actually attacked the Baptist choir and beat some of the singers. But the singers were out again the next year and were welcomed by many who were afraid to join them but greeted the worshipers thankfully, often with tears in their eyes.[2]

2. Joseph Ton, "The Traditional Christmas in Romania," *The Voice of Truth*, November-December 1982, p.1.

We do not suffer for our profession of faith in the one who came to earth that first Christmas. We have no bond in tribulation with those suffering ones in Romania and other places. But we are one with them all the same. Our experience is the same as theirs, and it is the same as that of the shepherds and the wise men and all who have found Christmas at whatever time and in whatever place. We have received the announcement. We have obeyed God's summons. We have found the Savior. We have worshiped Jesus.

> Come and worship, come and worship,
> Worship Christ, the newborn King.
> (James Montgomery)

II

The Gifts of Faith

IN MATTHEW we are told that some time after the birth
of Jesus Christ—perhaps as much as two years after the
event—wise men from the East came to worship Him. This
simple story has always figured largely in most celebrations of
Christmas, in this and other countries. Because it is an event
upon which the imagination may easily take hold, it has been
embellished widely both in literature and art.

From the Bible story we know very little about the wise
men. Millions of Christmas cards show three kings presenting gifts to a tiny child in a manger. People sing "We Three
Kings from Orient Are." But we do not know that there were
three wise men who brought the gifts. We are not told that
they were kings, or even when they arrived in Bethlehem. It
is likely, actually, in view of their long journey and of Herod's

command that all children under two years of age be killed, that they arrived when the infant Jesus had already become a young child.

The story is simplicity itself. "After Jesus was born in Bethlehem in Judea, during the time of King Herod, Magi from the east came to Jerusalem and asked, 'Where is the one who has been born king of the Jews? We saw his star in the east and have come to worship him.'" We are then told how the wise men inquired of Herod and how afterward, led by the star, they found the child in Bethlehem. "On coming to the house, they saw the child with his mother Mary, and they bowed down and worshiped him. Then they opened their treasures and presented him gifts of gold and of incense and of myrrh. And having been warned in a dream not to go back to Herod, they returned to their country by another route" (Matthew 2:1–2, 11–12).

The fact that so little information is given about the wise men clearly shows that Matthew's interest was not focused upon the wise men themselves. Rather, he was interested in the fact that Gentiles came to worship the Jewish Messiah, and in the gifts they bore. A literary critic would draw special attention to the gifts, for they occur at the end of the story after the child has been found and thus occupy a place of prominence.

METAL OF KINGS

It is easy to see why gold is an appropriate gift for Jesus Christ. Gold is the metal of kings. When gold was presented to Jesus it acknowledged His right to rule.

When I was driving through Greece, I found the kingly nature of gold reaffirmed in a striking way by archaeology. In the ruins of the town of Mycenae, which dates in its earliest strata from the time of the Trojan war, there is an ancient cemetery in which the kings of the towns were buried. Later in the archaeological museum at Athens I saw the objects found there, and among them gold was most prominent. One of the most precious finds of that period of Greek history is an elaborate death mask, called the mask of Agamemnon, done in pure gold. The same thing is illustrated by the elaborate burial ornaments discovered in the Valley of the Kings at Thebes in upper Egypt. This valley contained the coffin of King Tutankhamen as well as other golden objects from the same period of history.

It has often been pointed out that when the wise men brought gold to the infant Jesus they were being used by God to provide the funds necessary for Joseph to take the young child and His mother to Egypt to escape Herod's attempt on His life. That is probably true; but although it is true, it is far overshadowed by the significance of the gift itself. Jesus Christ was a king, as the wise men knew. He was the King of kings. The wise men pointed to His kingship with their gold.

INCENSE

It is also easy to see why incense was a significant gift. Incense was used in the Temple worship. It was mixed with the oil that was used to anoint the priests of Israel. It was part of the meal offerings that were offerings of thanksgiving and praise to God. Since incense gave the offering its pleasant odor, it was probably of incense that Paul was thinking when he compared the gifts of the Philippians to such a sacrifice, calling it "a fragrant offering, an acceptable sacrifice, pleasing to God" (Philippians 4:18). In presenting this gift the wise men pointed to Christ as our great High Priest, the one whose whole life was acceptable and well pleasing to His Father.

It is interesting that incense was never mixed with sin offerings. The meat and wine offerings were offerings for sin, and those were not to have incense mixed with them. Only the meal offerings, which were not for sin, were to receive the incense.

When we discover that, we think naturally of Jesus, to whom the incense was given. He was without sin. When His enemies came to Him on one occasion He challenged them with the question "Can any of you prove me guilty of sin?" (John 8:46). They were speechless. Earlier He had said of His Father, "I always do what pleases him" (John 8:29). None of us can say that. Since only the Lord Jesus Christ was sinless, it was extremely fitting that incense should have been offered to Him.

"We see from the symbolism of these gifts," wrote Donald Barnhouse early in his ministry,

> that the eternal royalty and holiness of Christ were announced from his earliest years. He had come forth from heaven to perform the work of redemption, and he was prepared in every way to do the Father's will so that he might fulfill every demand and obligation of the law. Thus only would he become eligible to die on the cross; and by that cross alone

redeem the world. That life could show that he was the fit candidate for the cross, and we cling with surety to the work that was accomplished there at Calvary, since we know that our sin-bearer was himself without sin.[1]

TOKEN OF DEATH

That observation leads naturally to the last of the gifts. For just as gold speaks of Christ's kingship and incense speaks of the perfection of His life, so does myrrh speak of His death. Myrrh was used in embalming. Because the trappings of death (although different) were as important then as today, myrrh was well known and was an important item of commerce.

We receive an idea of how important myrrh was in the ancient world as we read the Bible. For instance, for Jesus' burial Nicodemus used 100 pounds of myrrh and aloes to prepare the body. If 100 pounds of that combination were used for just one body, there must have been a tremendous amount of myrrh constantly being bought and sold for funeral arrangements. Moreover, in Revelation 2 we read of a city of Asia Minor called Smyrna. This name is actually the Greek word for myrrh. The city was called Smyrna because the manufacture of myrrh was its chief industry.

By any human measure it would be odd, if not offensive, to present to the infant Christ a spice used for embalming. But it was not offensive in this case, nor was it odd. It was a gift of faith. We do not know precisely what the wise men may have known or guessed about Christ's ministry, but we

1. Donald Grey Barnhouse, *The Gift of Death* (Philadelphia: American Bible Conferences Association, 1935), p. 5.

do know that the Old Testament again and again foretold His suffering. Psalm 22 describes His death by crucifixion; it was a verse from this psalm that Jesus quoted when He cried out from the cross "My God, my God, why have you forsaken me?" (Psalm 22:1; Mathew 27:46). Isaiah 53:4–5 says, "Surely he took up our infirmities and carried our sorrows, yet we considered him stricken by God, smitten by him, and afflicted. But he was pierced for our transgressions, he was crushed for our iniquities; the punishment that brought us peace was upon him, and by his wounds we are healed." Christ was to suffer, to die for sin. It was myrrh that symbolized this aspect of His ministry.

There were a few other uses of myrrh in the ancient world, one of which is particularly important here. It was a use of myrrh that the Lord Jesus Christ refused.

Every so often in the study of Scripture the student can learn a great lesson from verses that seem to contradict each other on the surface. On closer study they are actually seen to teach some truth. In Mark 15:23 and John 19:30 there is an example of such an apparent contradiction that actually teaches us something spiritual and makes sense only when we know about this additional use of myrrh. In the first verse we read that, when Jesus was crucified, the soldiers who performed the crucifixion offered Him wine mixed with myrrh and that He did not receive it. In the second verse we are told that later when some wine was again offered to Him He did receive it. What was the difference? The difference was that in the first case myrrh, which helped to deaden pain, was mixed with the wine. Since Jesus wished to bear all that suffering and death could bring to Him, when He had tasted the myrrh He turned away.

Later, in order to fulfill Psalm 69:21, which says, "They . . . gave me vinegar for my thirst," he called for something and drank what was offered. Myrrh was used to deaden pain. Jesus wished to suffer all that accompanied death when He died for us.

AN END TO SUFFERING

We have looked at the spiritual significance of each of the three gifts given to Jesus by the wise men: gold, incense, and myrrh. Gold for royalty! Incense for the purity of His life! Myrrh for suffering! Yet the study would be incomplete were we not also to see one other verse that bears upon the gifts of the wise men.

The verse is Isaiah 60:6 and occurs in the midst of a prophecy of the coming of Jesus Christ in glory at the end of this present age. The chapter begins: "Arise, shine, for your light has come, and the glory of the Lord rises upon you" (v. 1). It continues by showing that the nations shall come to Christ's light "and kings to the brightness of your dawn" (v. 3). Then comes verse 6. "Herds of camels will cover your land, young camels of Midian and Ephah. And all from Sheba will come, bearing gold and incense and proclaiming the praise of the Lord." Do you see the importance of this verse? When the Lord Jesus Christ returns, a scene will be enacted that is similar to the coming of the wise men to Bethlehem. He will reign in power. Gifts will be given to Him. But when the gifts are presented, they will be gold and incense only. Myrrh speaks of suffering, and when the Lord Jesus Christ died on the cross, He suffered once for all for sin. Hereafter there will be no more need for His suffering.

Jesus Christ came to earth to die for our sin. Now those who believe on Him wait for His second coming in glory.

Did you ever recognize that it was this truth—the truth that Jesus came to die but then rose from the dead to leave suffering behind forever—that led to the first Christian conversion? In the New Testament sense the first Christian was John, the author of the fourth gospel. Early on the first Easter Sunday morning after Jesus had risen from the dead, women came to the tomb, found the stone rolled away from the opening, and met the angels. They were puzzled by those things and sent one of their number to find John and Peter, who alone of the disciples remained in Jerusalem. On hearing the news, John and Peter went running to the burial site. John, the younger, arrived first. He stopped at the door and, looking in, saw the graveclothes in which the body of Jesus had been wrapped following the crucifixion. He did not understand that Jesus was risen.

While John hesitated at the door, Peter arrived, panting and out of breath, and immediately burst through the open door into the tomb. John entered cautiously behind. There in the tomb the odor of myrrh permeated everything. The graveclothes were there, now collapsed from the weight of the spices. The head cloth was there. The myrrh was there. But the body was gone. Suddenly John understood that Jesus had passed through the graveclothes, as He was later to pass through closed doors, and that He had indeed conquered death. He had been raised in a glorified body. When he understood that, John knew that the suffering of the Lord, symbolized by the myrrh, was finished forever.

It is a pity to miss the meaning of Christmas through ignorance, or, what is worse, to see it and understand it but fail to commit your life to the one who was born on that first Christmas in order that He might subsequently suffer for you and remove your sin forever.

The world has many false ideas of Christmas. For some persons it is only a story that is somehow meant to glorify babies and motherhood. For others there is the false idea that we must do something for God, like that ridiculous Christmas song "The Little Drummer Boy," which suggests that Jesus will smile on us if we play Him a tune. Jesus does not need us to play Him a tune. He does not need anything we can produce. But we do need Him! We need a Savior. That is why that great Christmas hymn by Charles Wesley says so clearly:

Come, though long-expected Jesus,
    Born to set Thy people free;
From our fears and sins release us;
    Let us find our rest in Thee.

Born thy people to deliver,
    Born a child, and yet a King.
Born to reign in us for ever,
    Now Thy gracious kingdom bring.

To understand Christmas is to understand that and come to Him in whom alone we have salvation.

OUR GIFTS

I have said that we can bring nothing to Christ, who alone is our Savior, but we must come with our faith. Moreover, there is a sense in which by faith we too may present our gifts of gold, incense, and myrrh.

Begin with your myrrh. Myrrh is not only a symbol of Christ's death but also of the spiritual death that should come to you for your sin. Lay it at Christ's feet, saying, "Lord Jesus Christ, I know that I am less perfect than You are and am a sinner. I know that I should receive the consequence of my sin, which is to be barred from Your presence forever. But You took my sin, dying in my place. I believe that. Now I ask You to accept me as Your child forever."

After you have done that, come with your incense, acknowledging that your life is as impure as the life of the Lord Jesus Christ is sinless. The Bible teaches that there is no good in man that is not mixed with evil. But it also teaches that Christ comes to live in the believer so that the good deeds produced in his or her life may become in their turn "a fragrant offering, an acceptable sacrifice, pleasing to God."

Finally, come with your gold. Gold symbolizes royalty. So when you come with your gold you acknowledge the right of Christ to rule your life. You say, "I am your servant; You are my Master. Direct my life and lead me in it so that I might grow up spiritually to honor and to serve You accordingly." Have you done that? Have you come believing in all that the myrrh, incense, and gold signify? If you have, you have embarked on a path of great spiritual joy and blessing. For those are the gifts of faith. They are the only things we can offer to the one who by grace has given all things to us.

12

RETURNING ANOTHER WAY

AN OLD CHRISTIAN tract entitled *Famous Last Words* was a collection of statements made by men as they were dying. Its point was that those last statements were important because they revealed whether the individual's philosophy of life was adequate. It set me thinking about the importance of many last words— words spoken by those who were dying, but also the last words of stories, poems, or novels. Some stories end, "And they lived happily ever after," a very significant closing. The Bible concludes by saying, "The grace of the Lord Jesus be with God's people. Amen."

That chain of thought came to me as I began to think about the verse "And having been warned in a dream not to go back to Herod, they returned to their country by another route" (Matthew 2:12). In particular, it came to me as I reflected on the last three words.

Those are the last words of the Christmas story after all. True, the account of the wise men coming to worship the young Christ child is followed by the warning of Joseph by the angel concerning Herod's plans and by the account of the flight of the young family to Egypt. But those events do not really seem to be a part of the Christmas story itself. Rather, they are an interlude between the story of the birth of Jesus and the appearance of John the Baptist as His forerunner approximately thirty years later. Everything else in the Christmas story comes before that statement—the announcement of the birth of John the Baptist to Zechariah, the announcement of the birth of Jesus to Joseph and Mary, the birth of both children, the appearance of the angels to the shepherds and their subsequent trip to the manger, finally the appearance of the star to the wise men, as a result of which they made their journey to Bethlehem. All that comes before the statement that the wise men returned to their country "by another route." So the phrase itself seems especially important. Why? Because it suggests that if anyone has truly seen and worshiped the Lord Jesus Christ, from that time on his way will inevitably be different. If you have met Him, your way will be different.

In looking at this phrase I want to look, first, at the difference it made in the lives of the wise men. Then, second and more important, I want to see the difference for us if we have actually seen and worshiped Jesus.

WISER WISE MEN

We are not told very much about the change in the wise men, for the story of those Eastern visitors breaks off with the verse we are studying. No doubt they went back as close to being real Christians as it was possible to be before the actual death and resurrection of the Lord. No doubt, too, the God who sent the star and later also spoke to them in a vision saw that they had sufficient illumination to believe on the Lord Jesus Christ as their Savior. Otherwise we must think that God directed them to Bethlehem merely to demonstrate a later turning of the Gentiles to Israel's Savior, entirely apart from His concern for them as persons. I doubt that. Still, as I say, we are not told those things specifically. That they were changed we do not doubt. We do not know how or to what degree.

Yet I do not think that we are entirely in the dark about the changes. We can see two just in the details of the story. First, the wise men had come to Jerusalem looking for a worldly, political king. The very fact that they came to Jerusalem indicates that. Jerusalem was the capital of the country, the seat of Herod's rule. When they came there, they were certainly expecting the child to have been born into Herod's family and the people of Judah to have been rejoicing at His birth. That was not what they found. Their own expectations directed them to the court at Jerusalem, but the child was actually in Bethlehem. They learned that from the prophecy that said,

> But you, Bethlehem, in the land of Judah,
>> are by no means least among the rulers of Judah;
> for out of you will come a ruler
>> who will be the shepherd of my people Israel.
>>> (Matthew 2:6; Micah 5:2)

Thus, although they came looking for a political king, they found a spiritual one. They found the one who would later

137

say to Pilate, Herod's successor, "My kingdom is not of this world. If it were, my servants would fight" (John 18:36). Can we doubt that at the very least the wise men returned with changed ideas concerning God's Messiah?

Moreover, they undoubtedly returned with changed views concerning this world's rulers. Herod had fooled them; for he had said that he wanted to worship the child when actually he wanted to murder Him—and they had believed Herod. They were only given to know his true character and intentions by God's warning in a dream.

They also had a new understanding of the chief priests and scribes, for they would have expected those religious leaders to be as interested in the object of their search as they themselves were, even more so since this was Israel's king. What they actually found was religious formalism and indifference. Those men knew where the Christ should be born, but they were not interested in traveling the five or so miles from Jerusalem to Bethlehem to worship Him.

Do you think that the wise men could have been insensitive to those great ironies? I hardly think so. Consequently, they must have returned to their own country profoundly changed men—changed in regard to the object of their worship and in their outlook on this world's rulers. That undoubtedly meant that they returned to their own country both literally and figuratively by another route.

THE WISE MEN'S WAY

The question I want to put to you at this point is whether you have had the experience of the wise men. Have you found

Jesus and had your way of life changed as a result? Or are you still going along in the same old way? Perhaps you have been looking for a political king or, to put it in more contemporary language, a secular solution to your problems. Perhaps you have been looking for success or money or sex to fill the God-created vacuum in your soul.

If you have, you need to learn that none of those things will do it. Only God can fill a God-vacuum. Consequently, you must come to God in Jesus. In his birth Jesus *revealed* God. In His death He *saved us* from our sin, dying in our place. In His resurrection he *provided proof* of the power available to us now to give victory over sin and one day transform us into His own holy and blessed image.

Perhaps you have been trusting in the wisdom of this world's rulers. You have followed this philosophy or that, and still you have not been satisfied. No wonder! In spiritual things God has made the wisdom of this world to be nothing. God's wisdom, the true wisdom, is revealed in the gospel of His Son, Jesus Christ. What He demands of you is that you meet Him there to learn of His wisdom and find salvation. Elsewhere you will only find His judgment. At the cross you find your sins covered by the blood of Christ's sacrifice and in place of judgment a full measure of God's great grace.

The first way, our way, is perilous. Romans describes our danger when it says, "Ruin and misery mark their ways, and the way of peace they do not know" (Romans 3:16–17). Jesus also described it when He said, "For wide is the gate and broad is the road that leads to destruction, and many enter through it. But small is the gate and narrow the road that leads to life, and only a few find it" (Matthew 7:13–14). On the other hand, the Bible says that God's way for us begins with Christ and that thereafter it is entirely just, true, pleasant, and perfect.

GOD'S WAY COMMENDED

May I commend this new way, the other way, to you? It is what you will find if you come first to Jesus.

I commend it, first of all, because it is a *definite* way. We read about it in the thirtieth chapter of Isaiah: "Whether you turn to the right or to the left, your ears will hear a voice behind you, saying, 'This is the way, walk in it'" (Isaiah 30:21). I wonder if you have seen how much we need a definite way in which to walk in this confusing world. Apart from a definite way we are all wanderers. Worse than that, we are lost entirely. We keep moving, of course, because we are unable to hold still; but we do not know where we are going or even where we should be going.

The Lord Jesus Christ tells us that He is the way (John 14:6); that is, He is the only way of salvation, the only way of access to the Father. Then, having told us of that great salvation, He sets a different and specific Christian way of life before us.

A definite way! That, of course, is why the early Christians were sometimes called those of the "the Way." They had been lost, but the way had been revealed to them. Now they were determined to walk in it by the grace of God.

I wish that all Christian ministers might be definite about pointing to that way, but I am afraid that many merely contribute to the confusion. Some years ago I heard about a guide in one of the British museums who was asked about one of the displays. "Which is Wellington and which is Napoleon?" the visitor asked.

"Whichever you please," the guide answered. "You have paid your money, and you may take your choice."

So it seems to be with many preachers and teachers in the church today. Not long ago I heard of a young seminarian who was being interviewed by a candidates committee of a certain presbytery. He seemed to be interested in the theological orientation of the men on the committee—too much so, in fact. After the interview was over and he had read his theological statement, someone asked him, "Why were you so interested in the theological orientation of the men on your committee?"

"I have three theological statements," he said. "One of them is liberal, one conservative, and a third neo-orthodox. I wanted to read the one the committee would be most pleased to hear." I do not doubt that approach will characterize the young man's ministry, as it characterizes the ministry of so many others. He will say what his listeners want to hear, but it will not be God's message. So, although he may be popular with the undiscerning to a degree, he will not be blessed by God, who, we are told, sets a definite way before all people.

Second, I can commend the way of God to you because it is a *perfect* way. It lacks nothing. True, at times it is hard to walk along it. We admit that. All life is hard at times. But this way is perfect nonetheless; for it is planned by the God who made us, knows us, loves us, and desires that we should become all that He has meant us to be.

That is taught in Psalm 18, where it is strikingly stated. The verses say that the way God sets before us is as perfect as His own way, which is obviously perfection itself. In verse 30 we read, "As for God, his way is perfect." Then, verse 32 continues, "God . . . makes my way perfect." Is the way of our own devising perfect? No. Otherwise we would not make so many mistakes. But God's way for us is perfect. That in itself should strongly commend that way to us.

Third, the way of God is an *assured* way. That is, it is a way guaranteed to get us to where we are going. Romans 6:22 says, "But now that you have been set free from sin and have become slaves to God, the benefit you reap leads to holiness, and the result is eternal life." When you set out on the king's way you inevitably get to the king's destination.

It would make a great deal of difference if believers as a whole would believe and appropriate that truth. So many Christians are uncertain about the Christian life. They take a step. But they are afraid, and so they step back again. They go forward. Then they wonder if it is right. They look around and haltingly take another step. That is not the way the Christian life is to be lived. The Lord tells us that He has set before us an assured way, one guaranteed to bring us into holiness of life now and the assurance of a full life with God hereafter. We should be confident as we walk with God—not in ourselves, of course, but confident in Him who has set such a perfect way before us.

Fourth, the new way is a *joyful* way. We see that in the Christmas story, for in each case we are told that those to whom God revealed the birth of Christ rejoiced at that great show of God's favor. When Mary had come to Elizabeth before the birth of John the Baptist, Elizabeth greeted her, saying that as soon as Mary's voice was heard "the baby in my womb [that is, John the Baptist] leaped for joy" (Luke 1:44). Mary responded, "My soul praises the Lord and my spirit rejoices in God my Savior" (vv. 46–47). Later the angel announced "good news of great joy that will be for all the people" (Luke 2:10), and the shepherds, who heard the tidings, went to find the Christ and afterward returned in great joy, "glorifying and praising God for all the things they had heard and seen, which were just as they had been told" (v. 20). Even the wise men were joyful; for we are told that "when they saw the star, they were overjoyed" (Matthew 2:10).

Have you known the joy of finding salvation in Christ and having the great questions of life answered in Him? Have you found the joy of knowing that God loves you? If not, you have not really known joy in the fullest sense, and I commend the way to you.

Finally, I commend the Christian way because it is *the only way*. I do not mean that there are not other sometimes very alluring ways that compete for our attention; there certainly are. I mean that it is the only way to God. If you are lost in the woods, there may be a dozen paths that will take you somewhere. But there is only one path that will take you directly back to your campfire and the fellowship of your friends. It is the same spiritually. There are many paths, but there is only one that will take you to God and will keep you in the way of blessing once you have found Him. The Lord spoke of that truth when He said, "I am the way and the truth and the life. No one comes to the Father except through me" (John 14:6). Do not insult God by trying to invent anther way; do not frustrate yourself by trying to do so. There is no other way. Other "ways to God" will end only in disappointment and ruin.

WALK YE IN IT

If you are a Christian, that is, one who has already come to God through Christ and who is therefore now trying to walk in the Christian way by God's grace, then keep on walking in it. There are sometimes difficulties in the Christian life. God sends some of them in order that we might be strengthened by them. But for every trial there is also a joy. For every discouragement there is a great reward. Do not give up. Allow the presence of Christ within your life to make the difference.

On the other hand, if you are not yet going in that way, you must do what the wise men did. The first thing they did was to seek Jesus. True, they had misconceptions about who He was, and they looked in the wrong places at first. But still, having heard of Him, they kept looking until the young child finally stood before them. There was much to discourage them: the great distance, their ignorance, and the disinterest of those who should have been pointing others to the world's Savior. But those things did not deter the wise men. They knew there was a Savior, and they were determined to have a part in Him. So they kept on until they saw him. Do not allow discouragement, ignorance, or disinterest to keep you from finding the Savior.

Moreover, having found Him, do not stop there. Do as the wise men did and go on to worship Him and serve Him. How can you worship Him? You can worship by acknowledging Him to be what He truly is: the everlasting God and your only Savior and Lord.

Is Jesus each of those things to you? Your God? Your Savior? Your Lord and King? He should be. He can be, right now. Will you give your life to Him? If you do, He will set such a glorious way before you that you will never want to return in the old way.

THE PEOPLE
OF
CHRISTMAS

13

SIMEON'S PSALM

I DO NOT KNOW who appeals to you most in the Christmas story, but as far as I am concerned, it is not one of the central characters. The Lord is an exception, of course. But apart from Him I find that the central characters—Mary and Joseph, perhaps even the wise men and the shepherds—are not the most interesting. The ones I find interesting are the minor people like Zechariah, Simeon, Anna, and all the unnamed people who are suggested in Luke 2 by the phrase "all who were looking forward to the redemption of Jerusalem" (v. 38).

It would be natural, looking at people only from a human point of view, to think first of Mary and Joseph, then of the wise men and shepherds, and after that the others. But I find in my experience that I have never yet been able to preach an exciting sermon about Joseph or Mary. I do better with the shepherds and the wise men. But the very best sermons, those I also enjoy most, are on the inconsequential people. When I say inconsequential, I am only using that word the way the world uses it. In God's sight they are not inconsequential at all. The really inconsequential people are Herod, Caesar Augustus, the scribes, the Pharisees, and the chief priests. The minor characters are important because they have so much faith.

Before I began to look into the matter, I believed that the people who lived in Christ's time probably had very little faith in His coming. That was true for many, of course. Certainly the world was in darkness at Christ's coming. The leaders obviously were not looking for Him. Jerusalem was insensitive. Yet as I read these stories I began to see that within Israel there were devout people who searched the Scriptures and understood from them that the Christ was to be born. Perhaps in studying the prophecy of Daniel they even had an indication that the time was at hand. Those godly people looked for Christ's coming and by the grace of God were enabled to see Him and recognize Him when He came.

That is very important, because it means that when God does His work He is not limited to those whom the world considers important (1 Corinthians 1:26–28). He has chosen the weak in order that He might bring glory to Himself.

GOD'S SENTINEL

We have a character like that in Simeon, whom Luke mentions in his second chapter. He does not tell us what Simeon's occupation was. We think occupation is important, but it does not concern God greatly. Luke does not tell us where Simeon lived. We are told nothing about his relatives. We are not told what his house looked like or whether he was rich or poor or well regarded or not well regarded. What we are told is that he was "righteous" (some translations say "just") and "devout," and that he waited for "the consolation of Israel" (v. 25).

I wish that could be said of God's people today—that they are all righteous and that they wait for the consolation of God's people.

To this man God had given a special revelation. He was close to God, so God was close to him. The Holy Spirit had worked in his life; God's Spirit had revealed to him that he would not see death until he should look upon the Lord's Christ. That means that he was somewhat of a sentinel, for he had been placed in Israel to point out the Christ when He came.

I think of an illustration from classical drama. In the play *Agamemnon* there is a scene in which a sentinel is perched on a hill to watch for the fire that will signal the destruction of Troy. When Troy fell, a fire was to be lit that could be seen by a sentinel stationed on a hill a reasonable distance away. He in turn was to light another fire that would be seen by another sentinel still farther away who would light a fire, and so on, fire after fire, until the message finally came all the away around the Aegean Sea to the palace of Agamemnon in the lower part of Greece. At the beginning of the play the sentinel is standing on his hill, the fire has not yet come, and he is bemoaning the captivity that is his by reason of this assignment. He says that the fall of Troy and the imprisonment of its people will mean his freedom.

While he is giving this speech, the fire appears, and he is released. The drama is set in motion.

Simeon was like that. He was looking for the Lord's Christ. I can imagine that every day as he went into the Temple area he must have looked about him to see if the Messiah had come. Is it this one? No! Is that the Christ? No! One day as he walked into the Temple he saw a poor couple—a man who was a carpenter in Nazareth and his wife, both of them probably quite young. They had a child, a tiny one just a month old. Immediately the Holy Spirit bore testimony to Simeon that this was the Savior.

Simeon did not look on the outward appearance. He did not say, "But, God, how can this be Your Messiah? I expected somebody much more important than this." No, he accepted the revelation as God gave it to him. So he walked over and, I suppose, introducing himself to Mary and Joseph, asked, "May I hold the child?" Then, holding the salvation of the world in his hands, he broke forth into these words of inspired song:

> Sovereign Lord, as you have promised,
> > you now dismiss your servant in peace.
> For my eyes have seen your salvation,
> > which you have prepared in the sight of all people,
> a light for revelation to the Gentiles
> > and for glory to your people Israel.
> (Luke 2:29–32)

The song is short, but it contains truths that testify to the understanding that this devout man had.

GOD'S SALVATION

Simeon spoke of the child's being God's salvation. We do not know what Hebrew word Simeon used. All we have is the Greek translation of what Simeon said. But it is significant that in the Greek text a special word for salvation appears. Simeon did not say, for instance, that God's *sōtēr* had been revealed, although *sōtēr* means "Savior." Nor did he say that God's *sōtēria* had been revealed. This word means "salvation." The word that occurs in the text is *sōtērion*, which means "one fitted to save." So, although it is true that the word certainly includes other meanings—the child was the "Savior" and the "salvation" of the world—the emphasis, it would seem, was on the fact that here at last was one fitted to do the saving work that nobody else could accomplish.

Why was He fitted to save? The answer is fourfold: He was God; He was man; He was sinless; and He was love.

It is quite important that He was God, because only God is equal to the needs of mankind. We are not equal to them. Even the greatest men are not equal to them. As a matter of fact, in our greatest moments we are still part of the problem, for we carry sin with us. Even when we would do good, evil abounds. What we need is a God equal to the problem of this world's sin.

Second, it is important that the child was true man, because only as a man could He die. It is hard to find an adequate illustration of this, but we can suggest it in this way. Years ago I knew a couple who wanted to do medical mission work. So they embarked on long years of preparation. First there was medical school itself. Then there was a residency. If we could have brought that couple before us and could have said to them, "But why are you doing all this preparation? Why are you spending four years in medical school and then four years in your residency? Why don't you simply go out to the field and do the job now?" they would have replied that the preparation was necessary if they were to do the work. Without the preparation they would not be equipped. In a similar way, if we were to turn to God Almighty and say, "But why didn't You just save men? Why did You go through the incarnation of Jesus?" God would reply, "But this is My preparation. It was necessary for My Son to become man in order that He might die."

It was also important that Christ be sinless. Only one who is himself sinless can die for others. If one of us should take it upon himself to do a work like that of the Lord Jesus Christ—if one should say, "Well, I'm magnanimous; I love everybody; I know that people are sinners and need a Savior, therefore I offer myself; I will die for the world"—the claim would be ludicrous. Each of us is a sinner and, therefore, we must die for our own sin if we die for anybody. But Jesus was sinless. He could die for others. Furthermore, being the infinite God, He could die for an infinite number.

Finally, He was love. This is important, for it would be possible, would it not, to have a God who was perfect, who became man, but who nevertheless was unwilling to die because he did not care for us and did not want to save us? Why should God save us, after all? Who are we? We have no claim upon Him. He can do without us. Yet the whole purpose of the incarnation, revealed in the message of the angel to both Mary and Joseph, is that Jesus had come to save His people from their sins. So when Simeon held the child in his arms and said, "At last I have seen God's salvation," he was saying, "Here is one who is perfectly suited to do what this world needs." He is God. He is man. He is sinless. He is the embodiment of the very love of God.

A DARK, DARK WORLD

Simeon said something else about Jesus—that He is "a light for revelation to the Gentiles." This is interesting, too, because the Gentiles of that day—and Israel also, to a large extent—were in gross darkness. I am sure that if you had gone to the palace of Herod and had said to him, "Is the Gentile world in darkness?" Herod would have said, "Of course not! The Gentile world is the Roman world, and Rome has brought light to barbarous people; the world is not in darkness." If you had asked the Greek philosophers, they would have said, "Perhaps in the case of the barbarians, but not the Greeks. We have our philosophy. We have Plato and Socrates and Epictetus and all of the others."

But if you should then go to the Scriptures and ask what God has to say, the answer is that not only was the world in darkness then, but the world is also in darkness today, apart from the light that the Lord Jesus Christ brings.

Paul spells it out in Romans 1. There Paul says that the problem is not that light is not available but that men have repressed the light and so have brought on their own darkness. God has revealed Himself in nature. But because men do not like the God revealed in nature, they have repressed that knowledge and so have turned from Him. Turning from the light they find themselves progressing into ever greater and greater darkness. "For although they knew God, they neither glorified him as God nor gave thanks to him, but their thinking became futile and their foolish hearts were darkened. Although they claimed to be wise, they became fools and exchanged the glory of the immortal God for images made to look like mortal man and birds and animals and reptiles" (Romans 1:21–23).

Paul also notes that rejection of God led them into many forms of immorality, including homosexuality. That is precisely the kind of world in which we live. It is a world that is getting darker and darker all the time.

The United States of America has had great light because of the gospel. We have a godly heritage. But America—let us be frank about it—is rejecting that light and has been for some time. Christmas is increasingly secular. I notice that even carols, if they have the gospel in them, are being eliminated from public life. Instead there are the superficial, supercilious jingles of our time. What our world is trying to do is gain an aura of religiosity, a good feeling at the Christmas season, while eliminating Christ. That is darkness, paganism, idolatry. The Lord Jesus Christ is the light necessary to enlighten the Gentiles.

GOD'S GLORY

Simeon also said that Jesus is "glory to [God's] people, Israel." In Greek the phrase is a genitive construction ("the glory of thy people, Israel"), and it could mean a number of things. It could be a subjective genitive, meaning that the part of the phrase following "of" is the subject of that which comes before. We have that in the phrase "the glory of the Lord"; it means that the Lord is the source of the glory. Again, it could be an objective genitive, in which case the word following "of" is the object. That is actually the case, for the phrase *the glory of Israel* means that a glory has been given to Israel. The Lord Jesus Christ is that glory.

Glory relates to God, for in the proper sense only He is glorious. Therefore, when Simeon held the Christ child in his arms he saw Him as God. He saw in the child the one who was also to be the world's Savior and therefore quite properly also the glory of God's own people, Israel.

Two Questions

I end with two questions. First, is Jesus God's light and glory to you? (Or is He just a story that you talk about at Christmastime? Has He illumined your darkness? Is He the one in whom you have seen and known God?) That is a most important question. If you do not know the answer, you can find out on the basis of whether or not you talk about Jesus, think about Jesus, and talk about Jesus with others. In every one of these stories, after the individuals had seen Christ and had received a revelation of who He was, they spoke of Him openly. When Christ has become our light, we find that so tremendous that we want to share it with the world. How can we keep silent when such a great revelation has been given?

The second question is this: If Christ is your light and glory, do you reflect His glory to others by the way you live?

That is what we are called to do. To be a Christian is to be a Christ-one, one in whom the Lord Jesus Christ can be seen. Can He be seen in you? You should be a mirror to reflect His glory. Or, to use another image, you should be a picture frame in which the Lord Jesus Christ is displayed. God is not too concerned whether you are a gold frame, and therefore valuable in the world's eyes, or whether you are just a simple wood frame like Simeon. All He is interested in is that you be an empty frame. For if you are empty of self, the Lord Jesus Christ may be placed there, and when men and women look at you, they will see the Lord.

14

The Little People of Christmas

THIS CHAPTER is about the least important person in the Christmas story. I have several reasons for writing it. For one thing, far too much attention is given to the people who are thought by the world to be important. I have noticed that people even like to identify with the wise men; but you hardly ever hear of people identifying with the "unimportant" people of the story.

Then, too, I think we often fail to see that it is generally those who are least important humanly speaking who are most important spiritually. That means that we can gain the greatest spiritual lessons by studying their lives, the things they learned, and the effect of the knowledge of God upon their characters. You remember how the apostle Paul stated this principle. He wrote, "God chose the foolish things of the world to shame the wise; God chose the weak things of the world to shame the strong. He chose the lowly things of this world and the despised things—and the things that are not—to nullify the things that are, so that no one may boast before him" (1 Corinthians 1:27–29).

My real reason for writing about the least important person in the Christmas story, however, is that Christmas is for the little people. That means it is for you and me. Christmas is not for the great of this world, at least not more than the others. It was not for the great in Christ's time. Caesar knew nothing of the birth of Jesus Christ. Neither did the Roman senate, the Greek philosophers, the generals. Not even the Jewish high priests or the members of the Sanhedrin knew of it. Christmas was for the people who were not important. It is for such people today.

THE LEAST IMPORTANT PERSON

You are probably wondering after this introduction just who is the least important person in the Christmas story. You can already guess from what I have said that it is not Caesar or Herod or the wise men. Since twelve verses are given to the wise men in Matthew's gospel, it is evident that Matthew thought they were of great significance.

Perhaps it was the shepherds. They were among the lowest social orders. No, they do not qualify either. Twelve verses of Luke's gospel are given to them. They were actually the most prominent persons of all on that first Christmas morning.

How about Simeon or Zechariah? No, not those either. Simeon is given a total of eleven verses by Luke, and the story of Zechariah together with the birth of his son, the future John the Baptist, takes up at least two-thirds of Luke's long first chapter.

Who is the least important character in the Christmas story? The least important person is one who receives only three verses in Luke's long account of Jesus' birth. And it is not even a man! It is a woman, and her name is Anna. Luke writes these words about her: "There was also a prophetess, Anna, the daughter of Phanuel, of the tribe of Asher. She was very old; she had lived with her husband seven years after her marriage, and then was a widow until she was eighty-four [or, for eighty-four years]. She never left the temple but worshiped night and day, fasting and praying. Coming up to them at that very moment, she gave thanks to God and spoke about the child to all who were looking forward to the redemption of Jerusalem" (Luke 2:36–38).

Here was a woman who was certainly the least of all the little people of the Christmas story. She was widowed. She was old—probably about one hundred five years old—to judge from Luke's figures. Yet from what Luke tells us, she undoubtedly understood more about the full significance of the coming of Jesus Christ than any of the others who appear in the nativity narratives.

REDEMPTION IN JERUSALEM

What was it that Anna the prophetess understood about the coming of Jesus Christ? Anna understood that the infant Jesus was to become the redeemer that God had promised to Israel. We know that because she announced His birth to all in Jerusalem who, like herself, looked for that redemption.

That was a remarkable thing. But we can only understand how remarkable it was when we realize fully what redemption means. The prefix of the word is *re*, which means "again"; and the main part of the word is based upon a root that means "to buy." Consequently, redemption is the act of buying something back, or the act of purchasing it again. We use the word in reference to repurchasing goods that have been left in a pawn shop. We redeem them. There is also a technical use of the word in business to describe the action of a company that is able to buy back various bond issues in order to cancel a financial obligation.

That is basic to the biblical meaning of the term. But there is an additional, special overtone to this word due to the fact that in biblical days it was used primarily for the act of freeing a slave. A slave could be set free if someone would pay the price necessary for his full redemption. In the various words that are used in the Bible for that type of redemption there is the suggestion that the person is "bought in the marketplace" (*agorazō*) where slaves were always sold, that he is "bought out of the marketplace" (*exagorazō*) never to be sold there again, and that he is "cut loose," or "set free" (*luō*). When the Bible uses the term in a spiritual sense it implies that although all have been sold under the slavery of sin and have been sold and resold as they have passed from one dealer in sin to another, Jesus Christ entered the marketplace in order to buy them back. He did so in order that the sinner might be purchased out of the marketplace forever.

In many parts of the Bible that idea is reinforced by references to the *price* paid for our redemption. Peter writes to his readers, "For you know that it was not with perishable things such as silver or gold that you were redeemed from the empty way of life handed down to you from your forefathers, but with the precious blood of Christ, a lamb without blemish or defect" (1 Peter 1:18–19). The price of our redemption was Christ's blood. We sing about it in one of our hymns.

> Nor silver nor gold hath obtained my redemption,
>> Nor riches of earth could have saved my poor soul;
> The blood of the cross is my only foundation,
>> The death of my Savior now maketh me whole.

> I am redeemed, but not with silver;
>> I am bought, but not with gold;
> Bought with a price—the blood of Jesus,
>> Precious price of love untold. (James M. Gray)

That is what Anna the prophetess was waiting for God to do for His people in the city of Jerusalem. So when she saw the infant Jesus she recognized Him as He who would one day pay the price of our redemption from sin and its power.

Christmas is not merely the story of the birth of a helpless baby in a stable, as beautiful as that may be, not the wonder of the shepherds, not the gifts of the wise men, not the enraptured singing of the angel chorus. The heart of Christmas lies in the fact that "God so loved the world that he gave his one and only Son, that whoever believes in him shall not perish but have eternal life" (John 3:16).

ONE OF MANY

Some may think it fantastic that Anna actually expected these things. But she did, and the fact is reinforced by Luke's statement that she was only one of many who looked for this redemption. Luke says that after she had seen Jesus she "spoke about the child *to all those who were looking forward* to the redemption of Jerusalem" (emphasis added).

I find that encouraging in light of what seems to be so much indifference to the claims of Jesus Christ today. The world of Christ's day was filled with those who were unaware of, or indifferent to, His coming—just as today. The Pharisees looked for a deliverer, but they were waiting for a leader who would enter Israel in power and drive out the occupying troops of the Roman army. Because of that fixed understanding of who the Messiah would be, the coming of Jesus as redeemer passed them by. There were also the Essenes. Those monklike figures looked for a teacher, a new Moses. But because Jesus did not come from their ascetic circles and teach their doctrines, they passed Him by. The Pharisees looked for a political Messiah. The Essenes looked for a teacher. The Sadducees looked for— nothing. But there were also believers, and those looked for a redeemer in Israel.

It had been the same in all the preceding ages. Why are the Old Testament saints in heaven today? Is it because they were Jews or had done good things? Or is it because they too looked for God's redeemer?

Abraham is in heaven today not because he left his home in Ur of the Chaldeans and went to Canaan; not because of his religion, his character, or his obedience. No, God promised him a great inheritance, and Abraham believed His promise about it. But the greatest promise Abraham believed was of the seed that should come from his line, through whom God would bring the blessing of salvation to all people and all nations. Abraham is in heaven because he believed God would do that.

How about Jacob? Why is he in heaven? Is it because of his religion, or because he was born in the line of his grandfather Abraham? Jacob is in heaven because he looked for a redeemer. Remember how he spoke about Him to his son Judah as he lay dying? "The scepter will not depart from Judah, nor the ruler's staff from between his feet, until he comes to whom it belongs and the obedience of the nations is his" (Genesis 49:10). Jacob is in heaven because he also looked for His coming.

David must be in heaven because of his character. After all, he was called "a man after God's own heart."

"My character!" David would say. "Are you forgetting that I committed adultery with Bathsheba and then tried to cover it over by having her husband killed? I'm in heaven because I looked for one who was promised as my redeemer and the redeemer of my people. I knew that God had promised Him a kingdom that would endure forever."

What about Isaiah? Did he expect the redeemer?

Of course he did. Isaiah prophesied, "Surely he took up our infirmities and carried our sorrows. . . . he was pierced for our transgressions, he was crushed for our iniquities." Isaiah knew that the Lord would lay on Messiah "the iniquity of us all" (Isaiah 53:4–6).

That has always been the faith of God's children, and for that reason the redeeming work of Jesus has always been found at the heart of the Christmas story. The angel said, "You are to give him the name Jesus, because he will save his people from their sins" (Matthew 1:21). In every age God has always had those who looked for this Savior. In ancient times there were Abraham, Jacob, David, Isaiah, Malachi, and more. In Christ's time there were Zechariah, John the Baptist, Joseph, Mary, Simeon, Anna, and others. There are millions of believers today. Are you one? Do you know Christ as your Redeemer? How sad it would be if you could manage to go through another Christmas without coming to believe in Him who came to earth, not to remain in a cradle but to die for you, to enrich your life now through His own indwelling Spirit and eventually to bring you with great joy into heaven.

TELLING OTHERS

There is one more thing we need to notice about this remarkable woman Anna. Luke tells us that after she had seen Jesus she *spoke about the child* to all who were looking forward to the redemption of Jerusalem" (Luke 2:38, emphasis added). As the shepherds had earlier, she became a witness to all that she had seen and heard. That was the apex of her spiritual perception. She spoke of Him! Do you? Are you a witness to Jesus Christ? You should be, if you know Him.

It is evident that Anna would never have been able to speak of Jesus to those who were looking for God's redemption unless she had previously come to know who they were. She was not the kind of believer that detached herself from the world, even though she spent all her time in the Temple. She was one who knew people. And she knew them well enough to be aware of their own deep spiritual longings. Because of her knowledge God used her to tell them about Jesus.

God needs such servants today. Never forget that while you are thrilling to Christmas with all the joy that comes from knowing Jesus, there are others, perhaps as close as the house next door or perhaps in your own home, who do not know Him and for whom these weeks lack all spiritual significance. There is the neighbor caught up in his business, becoming more and more frantic as the pre-Christmas shopping days draw to a close, but inwardly empty and wondering if there is anything better in life than his business. There is the widow who has recently lost her husband, or the parents who have recently lost their only son. They do not know Jesus, and they have no real joy or comfort. There are the lonely, the disappointed, the frustrated, the disillusioned, the abandoned members of our society—all longing for something better and yet not knowing what that something is. For them Christmas will be merriment without joy, glitter without the inner sparkle of the soul, frenzy without lasting satisfaction. These need Jesus Christ. But they need someone to know them and tell how He is the answer to their longings. You will never win these people for Jesus until you know them well enough for them to have shared their spiritual longings.

There is one more thing. You must also *tell* them about Christ and His redemption. Anna did not only know the persons who looked for redemption; she also spoke to them about Jesus. She became His first great witness in Jerusalem.

Is it not interesting that the life of Jesus Christ begins and ends with the great commission? It begins here with Anna. It ends with Jesus telling His disciples, "Therefore go and make disciples of all nations, baptizing them in the name of the Father and of the Son and of the Holy Spirit, and teaching them to obey everything I have commanded you. And surely I will be with you always, to the very end of the age" (Matthew 28:19–20).

If we really understand what Christmas is all about, we will do that and do it with joy. We will rejoice that God has revealed Himself to us, the little people, and given us the task of telling others about Him.

15

How to Celebrate Christmas

LUKE 2:17–20 TELLS how to celebrate Christmas. How should we celebrate Christmas? The question is important because of the importance of the day and because so many obviously do not know how to celebrate it.

We know, of course, that Jesus was probably not born on December 25—at least there is no real evidence that He was. Nevertheless, this is the day that most people, Christians and non-Christians alike, observe as His birthday, and if we are to mark it at all, this seems to be the only realistic time to do it. But how? That is the question. What is a genuinely Christian way to observe Christ's nativity? Quite obviously, the fact that the world often celebrates the day in non-Christian ways is no excuse for Christians to either neglect or misuse it.

How do you celebrate Christmas? If we are honest, we must admit that many persons, even Christians, celebrate it most by watching football games on television, decorating their houses, visiting relatives and friends, or buying presents. Others—I hope Christians are not among this number—celebrate it by getting drunk, some beginning at the office party on the last working day before Christmas and not sobering up until sometime after the twenty-fifth or even after New Year's. That, of course, is monstrous. The other ways are inadequate.

But how should a Christian celebrate Christmas?

Before we turn to our text we need to say first that by far the best and greatest way to celebrate Christmas is by becoming a Christian if you have never done so. In other words, the best way to celebrate Christmas is by becoming a follower of Him whose birth we commemorate. It has to do with why Jesus came. The Bible tells us that the birth of Jesus was unlike all other births in that Jesus existed before birth as the second Person of the Godhead and that He became man, not to provide us with a sentimental story to tell children each winter, or as a theme for great musical compositions, but in order to grow to maturity and then to die for our sin as the means of our salvation. Jesus was born to be our Savior, as the carol says:

Good Christian men, rejoice
With heart and soul and voice!
Now ye need not fear the grave;

Jesus Christ was born to save!
Calls you one and calls you all
To gain His everlasting hall.
Christ was born to save!
Christ was born to save!

Anyone can understand Christmas by just three propositions: (1) I am a sinner; (2) as a sinner I need a Savior; (3) Jesus is that Savior. Three propositions! Hence, the best way to celebrate Christmas is to believe on Jesus as your Savior. If you have never done that, then Christmas is a great season in which to believe on Him.

But now, assuming that you have believed on Him and that you are a Christian, what can you add to this in order to celebrate Christmas properly? At this point our text comes in, for it is a report of how those who witnessed the first Christmas observed it. The passage begins by speaking of the shepherds: "When they had seen him, they spread the word concerning what had been told them about this child, and all who heard it were amazed at what the shepherds said to them. But Mary treasured up all these things and pondered them in her heart. The shepherds returned, glorifying and praising God for all the things they had heard and seen, which were just as they had been told" (Luke 2:17–20).

The means of celebrating Christmas this passage suggests are: (1) to tell others about it; (2) to wonder at the event itself; (3) to ponder its meaning; and (4) to glorify and praise God for what was done there. We need to think about each one.

GOOD NEWS

In the first place, we are told that after the shepherds had come to Bethlehem and had seen the infant Jesus, they "spread the word" about what was told them concerning the child. In other words, the shepherds became witnesses of the event. The reasons they became witnesses are that there *was* an event, a great event, and that others very much needed to hear of it.

Can we doubt that the shepherds had something worth telling? Hardly! For if their story was not worth telling, then no story that has ever been told is worth telling, and life is lacking in all joy and meaning. What had happened to these men? They had been out in the fields of Bethlehem in the middle of the night, watching over their sheep as they had for many hundreds of nights previously and as their fathers undoubtedly had before them. They had no thought for spiritual things—at least we are not told that they did—and they certainly did not expect the miracle. But then, suddenly, an angel appeared with the message: "Do not be afraid. I bring you good news of great joy that will be for all the people. Today in the town of David a Savior has been born to you; he is Christ the Lord" (Luke 2:10–11). After the angel had spoken, there appeared a host of angels all praising God and saying, "Glory to God in the highest, and on earth peace to men on whom his favor rests" (Luke 2:14). When the angels had departed the shepherds decided to go to Bethlehem. So they left their flocks and came and found Jesus, precisely as the angels had indicated. What they had been told coincided with their own experience, and they could not resist speaking of such things.

These men, poor shepherds though they were, had seen God incarnate. They had heard the music of heaven. They had seen the angels and had come to worship the angels' King. How could their tongues be silent when they had heard such music? How could they refuse to tell what they had seen?

Moreover, not only did these men have something to tell, as we also do, but the shepherds also knew of a world that needed desperately to hear their message. It was a sad world in their time. It was lost, confused, dying. It was lost because it lacked direction, primarily spiritual direction. It was confused because it lacked revelation and therefore also an awareness of truth. It was dying because it had no adequate cause for which to live. The world of the shepherds' day was much like the world of our day, in which the lamps of knowledge and culture seem to be slowly flickering out.

But over against that dying world there was Jesus. Later in His life He would speak of Himself in precise relationship to the world's condition. He would say that He was "the way"—for a world that was lost; He was "the truth"—for a world that was dreadfully confused; He was "the life"—for a world that was dying. The Way! The Truth! The Life! The shepherds took the message, in the only form they knew, to their contemporaries. That is the perfect combination, then—a knowledge of the good news (which is only another name for the gospel) and the people who need to hear it. That combination, when truly understood and seized upon, produces witnesses.

Would anyone want to say that those men were not authorized to spread such a message? Will anyone argue that they were uneducated? Or that they had not been endorsed by the Temple authorities? If anyone would argue in that way, let him notice that they had the most important authorization of all—possession of good news that had been revealed to them by God. Anybody who knows good news is authorized to tell it, particularly when it is news that will be the means of the salvation of others. The Scriptures say, "Let him who hears say, 'Come'" (Revelation 22:17). In other words, the only ultimate essential for proclaiming the gospel is a knowledge of it. So every one who knows Christ and has become a Christian can tell others of Him.

Here then is the first way to celebrate Christmas, as suggested by these verses. Imitate the shepherds in spreading the word about Jesus.

AMAZEMENT

The second way you and I can celebrate Christmas is to be amazed at it. That is suggested in Luke 2:18—"And all who heard it were amazed at what the shepherds said to them."

There are two kinds of amazement, of course, and to be perfectly fair we must admit that at the beginning. One kind of amazement is merely a tickling of the fancy. It is what we call a seven-day wonder; that is, a temporary fascination with something unusual. After such a wonder has run its course nobody gives the cause of it a second thought, and rightly so. The other kind of amazement is quite different. It is a holy amazement, which is a proper wonder at those acts of God that are beyond human comprehension. It borders on adoration if, indeed, it is not identical to it.

In one sense all the acts of God are legitimate grounds for such amazement. If we turn back to the earliest chapters of

Genesis, we discover a description of the globe before God fashioned it into the kind of world we know now and are told that in that period "the Spirit of God was hovering over the waters" (Genesis 1:2). What a cause for wonder that is! Then out of the darkness God spoke to call forth life and order. We turn from that picture to the final pages of the Bible, and in those pages we find the Lord Jesus Christ high and lifted up and all created orders paying homage to Him. That is a cause for wonder. From beginning to end God's dealings with our race are a cause for amazement. But of all those dealings, that which should evoke our greatest amazement is the incarnation of the Son of God, which we mark especially at Christmas. God become man! The Deity in human flesh! How can that be? We cannot understand it; but it is true nevertheless, and we marvel at it. Or at least we should marvel at it.

Do you want to celebrate Christmas? Then be amazed at it. Allow it to stretch your mind.

I believe that is why the wonder of children seems so appropriate at Christmastime. It is not that their wonder is all a Christian wonder, of course. They are not all thinking of God or Jesus as they stand spellbound at the presents and tree on Christmas morning. Or at least that is not the whole of their wonder. But their wonder is not inappropriate, for at the very least it is an analogy of what our wonder should be if we are those who (at least in part) understand the Christmas story.

So let the learning be two ways. Children must learn who Jesus is and what Christmas is all about from us. They must learn to love Him and serve Him more and more acceptably. But let us also learn from them and so recapture our own sense of amazement at the incarnation. That is the second way to celebrate Christmas.

MARY PONDERED

The third way in which you and I can celebrate Christmas is to ponder it, for Mary, we are told, "treasured up all these things and pondered them in her heart" (v. 19). Pondering is connected with amazement, of course, for it begins with it. But it also goes beyond amazement as an attempt to understand the mystery or figure it out. It implies a diving beneath the surface. It involves an effort to enter into the heart and counsels of God. Do that. Spend some time at Christmas thinking over what you know of God and trying to understand the ways of God more fully.

May I add one other thought to that? Pondering is work. It is not just brooding or getting into a pious frame of mind. It is an attempt to take what you know and then by an exercise of the mind to build upon it. Think what it involved in the case of Mary, Jesus' mother. First, it involved her memory; for we are told that she "*treasured up* all these things." Second, it involved her affections, for she "treasured up all these things . . . *in her heart*." Third, it involved her intellect; for she "treasured up all these things and *pondered* them in her heart."

Can you do that as a Christian? Of course, you can. You can remember the events. You can remember the moment in which they became real for you personally. You can sharpen up your affections; indeed, you must, for it is a terrible thing to have your love for the one who is the Lord of love grow cold. Then you can think about these things and allow God to teach you more about Himself. Our time is poorly spent if we allow daily affairs to eclipse times of pondering upon God's Word.

PRAISE AND GLORY

Finally, the text suggests that we can celebrate Christmas by glorifying God and by praising Him: "The shepherds returned, glorifying and praising God for all the things they had heard and seen, which were just as they had been told" (v. 20). To do that is to worship God both by words and in song.

I love the word *glory*, or *glorify*. It is one of the great words of the Greek language. Long ago, when that language was in its infancy, the word from which *glory* came meant "to have an opinion." Later it came to mean only "to have a good opinion." Finally, by an obvious extension, it meant a person's true "worth." The noun form of the word is *doxa*, which we have in our words *orthodox*, *heterodox*, and *paradox*. Those words mean "a right opinion," "a wrong opinion," and "a contradictory opinion" respectively.

When you acknowledge a person's true worth, which is only another way of saying that you express a proper opinion of him, you may be said to be glorifying him. That is the sense in which we glorify God. Moreover, since acknowledging His true worth is the essential meaning of worship—it means to acknowledge God's worth-ship—to glorify God is to worship Him by words. It is in that sense a doxology, which means to express a right opinion of God verbally.

That is what the shepherds did, and we are to imitate them. You can tell if you do by attempting to rehearse God's attributes. What are they? The birth of Christ itself teaches us of God's love; for God loved us so much that He became man in order to die for us. It also teaches us God's power, for an incarnation is beyond our ability even to imagine, let alone to bring into being. In the birth we see God's wisdom. We learn of His mercy. We see His disposition to use little things, to exalt the humble, and to subdue the proud. We see His grace. Have you seen those things and confessed them to God and others?

You can do that in song. For praising God is essentially an act of glorifying God with the whole being, and, in this, music quite naturally takes a part. That is why carols are so much a rightful part of Christmas; for, when sung by those who understand them, they are a means of praise.

> Hark! the herald angels sing,
> "Glory to the newborn King."

> Joy to the world! the Lord is come.

> O come, all ye faithful,
> Joyful and triumphant,
> O come ye, O come ye to Bethlehem;
> Come and behold Him
> Born the King of angels;
> O come, let us adore Him,
> Christ the Lord.

GOD'S GLORY

If those four means of celebrating Christmas seem right to you, and if you want to put them into practice, I suggest that you begin not with the first verse (v. 17) but with verses 18, 19, and 20. Verse 17 says that we are to tell others what we have seen and heard; but we can hardly do that effectively until we have first been amazed at Christ's birth, pondered its meaning, and glorified and praised God for it. You cannot tell that which you have not first felt and experienced.

So begin by wondering—wondering at the fact that you have not suffered the just punishment of your sin, that God has loved you, that Jesus came and died for you, that God called you to faith in Himself when you were yet without hope of salvation, and that you are now God's child and are secure in His love. Continue by thinking upon those things. Ponder the great doctrines of the Christian faith—doctrines of the incarnation, atonement, grace, sanctification, heaven, perseverance, and others—so that you begin to grow strong in doctrine. Glorify and praise God for what you know. Sing God's praises. Then, when you have done that and are qualified to speak, go back and tell others.

Furthermore, do not think that you need to go back to church in order to do those things, but learn rather to do them wherever God sends you—in your home, school, business. That is what the shepherds did. We are told that they "returned," glorifying and praising God. To what did they return? Why, to their sheep, obviously. And there, where they had first heard the angels' song, they themselves were heard to be singing God's praise.

May God give you grace to do that. If you and I and all others who call upon the name of our God should do it, the whole world would rightly resound with His praise.

16

THE INDESCRIBABLE GIFT

THERE ARE SEVERAL REASONS you or I might be unable to describe a Christmas gift. We might be overcome with emotion so that "words fail us," as we say. Or we might be unable to identify the gift. We might open it (as my father opened a gift on one occasion) and say, "It's beautiful—just what I always wanted. Uh—what is it?" Or we might care so little for a gift that we might not even bother to describe it.

Our failures would not make the gift indescribable, however, for there would always be someone else who could do what we failed to do. The salesperson could describe it, and probably did. So could the manufacturer. If it is a large or well-known gift, many others might get into the act. Some years ago Richard Burton, the actor, gave Elizabeth Taylor the largest diamond that anyone (except a king) had ever given anybody. It was a superlative present, worth millions of dollars. But it was not indescribable! On the contrary, it was described in every newspaper in the country so that soon nearly everyone knew the diamond's size, color, shape, weight, and value.

What can possibly make a gift indescribable? Since all human presents are describable, it is clear that the only thing that can make a gift indescribable is that it is more than human. It has to have something of God mixed with it. And, of course, that was precisely Paul's thinking when he penned 2 Corinthians 9:15. He had been thinking of very human gifts: the gifts of the Corinthians to the poor in Jerusalem. But the subject of giving had turned his mind to God and the gift of Christ to His people, which is the greatest of all possible gifts, and Paul ended his comments by referring to that divine bounty. He said, "Thanks be to God for his indescribable gift!"

That text contains only eight words, yet it points beyond words. It points to a gift that, if we have it, makes us richer than any merely secular king and happier than any earthly potentate.

GOD WITH US

When Paul speaks of Jesus as God's "indescribable gift" it is evident that he is not merely toying with words or exaggerating by an undisciplined use of superlatives. He is only saying what is patently true and is as true for us as it was for him. Who has been able to describe the gift of salvation from God in Christ? Painters have tried. Some of the most beautiful paintings in the world are of the Holy Family or Madonna and Child. My spirit soars when I look at a Raphael Madonna or stand silently before a nativity work by Fra Filippo Lippi. But I know that, however beautiful those works may be, they do not do justice to their subject. And the painters knew that too, else they would not have continued to paint masterpieces.

Musicians have tried to describe Christ's coming. By general acclaim there are probably no grander attempts to do this in all history than George Frederick Handel's *Messiah*, with its glorious "Hallelujah Chorus," or Johann Sebastian Bach's *Christmas Oratorio*. But glorious as those compositions are, I cannot believe they match even the angel chorus above the fields of Bethlehem, not to mention that full chorus of the praise of the redeemed recorded in the book of Revelation. Even those final choruses in Revelation fall short of describing God's gift, for it is necessary for those who sing them to continue day and night and never stop singing:

> To him who sits on the throne and to the Lamb
> be praise and honor and glory and power,
>> for ever and ever! . . . Amen!
>> (Revelation 5:13–14)

Have poets described the gift of God to perfection? Obviously not. John Milton wrote:

> Welcome all wonders in one sight—
>> Eternity shut in a span,
> Summer in winter, day in night,
> Heaven in earth, and God in man.
>> Blest little one,
>> Whose all embracing birth
> Lifts earth to heaven, stoops heaven to earth.

I do not know of any verse that packs more good theology into less space with more suggestive wording than this stanza, but these words also fall short of describing the indescribable, as all efforts must.

Why is the gift of God beyond description? There are several reasons, and the first is *the nature of the gift itself*. The gift is Christ. So, in order fully to describe this gift we must be able fully to describe who Jesus is and what He has done for our salvation, which we cannot do. Think of the difficulties involved in unfolding just that first part: who Jesus is. Jesus described Himself as being one with God the Father, and the Scripture everywhere testifies to that fact. Even His name, *Jesus*, means "*Jehovah* saves." *Immanuel* means "God with us." If Jesus is God, we cannot describe Him because God Himself is indescribable. Can we say what it means for God to be self-existent, having no origins and being beyond the full range of human discovery? Can we say what it means for Him to be self-sufficient, needing nobody? Can we understand what it means to be a spirit or to be "infinite, eternal, and unchangeable," as the Westminster Shorter Catechism states the matter? Those things are beyond us, so much so that even God (I say it reverently) cannot fully describe Himself when speaking to mere human beings. When Moses asked God who he should say God was, God answered, "I am who I am. This is what you are to say to the Israelites: 'I AM has sent me to you'" (Exodus 3:14).

We have another problem if we attempt to describe God: we cannot understand the Trinity. Jesus claimed to be God, but at the same time He spoke of God the Father and prayed to Him, thus indicating that there were distinctions of Persons within the Godhead. How are we to get a handle on that? We even have difficulty finding language that does not somehow inevitably err when we attempt to describe what the Trinity means. In fact, it took the church more than three hundred years—from the death of Christ to the Council of Constantinople (A.D. 381)—before it finally ratified the formula of one God existing in three co-equal persons. But even that only kept the church from erroneous statements; it did not exhaust the meaning of the Trinity.

Again, Jesus is not only God. He is man as well, and we cannot adequately describe the incarnation. The formula by which the Trinity is set off from error came out of the Council of Constantinople in A.D. 381. But it was another eighty years before the Council of Chalcedon produced language to describe the Lord's dual nature (A.D. 451). This council spoke of Christ's being

> perfect in Godhead and also perfect in manhood; truly God and truly man, of a reasonable [rational] soul and body; consubstantial [coessential] with the Father according to the Godhead, and consubstantial with us according to the Manhood; in all things like unto us, without sin; begotten before all ages of the Father according to the Godhead, and in these latter days, for us and for our salvation, born of the Virgin Mary, the Mother of God, according to the Manhood; one and the same Christ, Son, Lord, Only-begotten, to be acknowledged in two natures, inconfusedly, unchangeably, indivisibly inseparably; the distinction of natures being by no means taken away by the union, but rather the property of each nature being preserved . . .

Briefly put, the creeds state that there is one God in three persons and that Jesus is one person in two natures. But that does not adequately describe God's gift. At best it only keeps us from errors when we think about Him.

Even that is not all we must face when we think of trying to describe God's gift. For the gift consists not merely of who Jesus Christ is, which we have been discussing, but also of *what He has done*. Jesus came to provide salvation for us by His sacrifice on the cross, and we cannot adequately describe that, either. God has given us terms by which to understand it. We have words like *sacrifice*, *atonement*, *propitiation*, *reconciliation*. But how did Jesus achieve reconciliation by dying? Take His great cry of dereliction from the cross: "My God, my God, why have you forsaken me?" (Matthew 27:46). What does that mean? Had God actually forsaken Jesus? Was there some kind of temporary division within the Godhead? Or was Jesus only abandoned in the sense that He was given up to death rather than being delivered from it?

One year, during a question-and-answer period at the Philadelphia Conference on Reformed Theology, someone asked that question, and a number of the speakers for that particular conference responded. The first toyed with the question without saying very much—at least in my opinion. I was next; I said that, yes, although I could not explain how it was possible, I did believe that God the Father turned His back on God the Son at the moment He became sin for us and that Jesus in that moment endured the fullness of spiritual death on our behalf. But then Dr. Roger R. Nicole, the most distinguished theologian among us, rose and said flatly, "There can never be a division in the Godhead." Few could miss that even in one particular branch of Christian theology, the theology of the Reformation, and even among men who very much see eye to eye on most matters, there was evidently a limitation of understanding by all of us in that area.

The nature and work of the Lord Jesus Christ are beyond our full understanding, and therefore also beyond our powers of description.

WHILE WE WERE SINNERS

But the gift of God is also indescribable because of *the grace by which it is given*. Most of our gifts have nothing to do with grace. We give because the recipients of our gifts have some claim upon us: they are members of our family, people who have helped us in some way, or individuals who gave to us last year. Even when we give to someone who has no special claim upon us, someone who is perhaps just in great physical or material need, we usually do so because of some recognized obligation due to both of us being members of the human race. But God is not a member of the human race, and our race is in rebellion against Him. We are His enemies. Yet it was "while we were still sinners [enemies] Christ died for us" (Romans 5:8).

One of the books in my library is an anthology of master sermons from the Reformation to our own day, compiled by Andrew W. Blackwood, former professor of homiletics at Princeton Theological Seminary. It contains a sermon on this theme by the original speaker on "The Lutheran Hour," Walter A. Maier.

The great gift of Christ is granted not to God's friends, but to his enemies, to those who in their sins have risen up against God and declared war against the Almighty. To every one of us, suffering, as we and our world are, under the destructive powers of sin, God offers his gift of "unspeakable" grace. Christmas does not offer rejoicing to a selected few; it cries out, "Joy to the world!" We stand before that supreme and saving truth, the holy of holies of our Christian faith, the blessed assurance that "Christ Jesus came into the world," not to build big and costly churches, not to give his followers earthly power and rule, but—and this is why the angels sang their praise—"to save sinners." He came, not to establish social service, social consciousness, social justice, but first and foremost he came to seal our salvation.

No wonder that the apostle calls the mercy of God as shown by the gift of Christ "unspeakable"; it goes beyond the limit of human speech. Just as beholding the glare of the sun, men lose their power of vision, so raising our eyes to the brilliance of Jesus, the Sun of Righteousness, we are blinded by the splendor of the greatest Gift that God himself could bestow. Christ came to save—blessed assurance! But more: he came to "save . . . to the uttermost," so that no sin is too great, no sinner too vile, to be blessed, when penitent and believing, by this Gift.[1]

It is not only the gift but also the gracious manner in which the gift is given that exceeds our powers of description. Reason falters, logic fails, oratory stammers when confounded by this mystery.

1. Walter A. Maier, "Thanks Be unto God for His Unspeakable Gift!" in Andrew Watterson Blackwood, comp., *The Protestant Pulpit: An Anthology of Master Sermons from the Reformation to Our Own Day* (1947; reprint, Grand Rapids: Baker, 1978), p. 234.

What I Owe

A third reason the gift of God is indescribable is the *effects it produces*, which are unmeasurable by human beings.

The gift of God accomplishes everything in those who believe. First, Jesus brings forgiveness of sins, according to the riches of God's grace. We are in rebellion against God, and God has loved us while we were yet sinners. But God does not merely love us and let it go at that. He also forgives our sin through Christ's sacrifice. That means removal of sin so far as God is concerned. The Bible tells us that God hurls "all our iniquities into the depths of the sea" (Micah 7:19). It says, "I have swept away your offenses like a cloud, your sins like the morning mist" (Isaiah 44:22). David wrote, "As far as the east is from the west, so far has he removed our transgressions from us" (Psalm 103:12). The Bible says, "Their sins and lawless acts I will remember no more" (Hebrews 10:17; cf. Jeremiah 31:34). God knows everything, but according to this verse the only thing He has ever forgotten is the sins of those who believe that Jesus died for them. If we have received God's gift, we do not need to fear that our sins will ever rise up again to haunt us.

Second, the believer in Christ is justified before the bar of God's justice. Forgiveness is a negative thing; it forgets the past. Justification is positive; it brings a new standing before God that we did not have before and could never have achieved for ourselves. The Bible speaks of it as being clothed with the righteousness of Christ, as with a new suit of clothes. Before, we were clothed with the filthy rags of our own righteousness. Those are taken off, and we are given new garments.

Third, we are adopted into God's family. Before, we were of no family. We were "separate from Christ, excluded from citizenship in Israel and foreigners to the covenants of promise, without hope and without God in the world" (Ephesians 2:12). But now, "how great is the love the Father has lavished on us, that we should be called the children of God!" (1 John 3:1). As children we have the privilege of coming to God at any time with any matter, knowing that He cares for us as a father cares for a beloved son or daughter and that He will always answer our requests according to His own great wisdom.

Fourth, as God's children we are God's heirs. Paul writes, "If we are children, then we are heirs—heirs of God and co-heirs with Christ" (Romans 8:17). The word *co-heir* means that we possess all things jointly with Christ. All things! That is clearly indescribable.

Fifth, we have the gift of the Holy Spirit who unites us to Christ forever. That makes our bodies temples of God, who dwells in us.

Sixth, we have a divine peace that goes beyond circumstances and is beyond any poor human efforts to describe. Paul calls it a peace "which transcends all understanding" (Philippians 4:7). That is a priceless blessing in the midst of the sorrows that habitually overtake us in this life.

Seventh, we have a home in heaven prepared for us by Christ. Just before His crucifixion Jesus said to His disciples, "Do not let your hearts be troubled. Trust in God; trust also in me. In my Father's house are many rooms; if it were not so, I would have told you. I am going there to prepare a place for you. And if I go and prepare a place for you, I will come back and take you to be with me that you also may be where I am" (John 14:1–3). The Scottish preacher Robert Murray McCheyne wrote a hymn in which he looked over the benefits of God's salvation and then ahead to heaven, saying:

> When this passing world is done,
> When has sunk yon glaring sun,
> When we stand with Christ in glory,
> Looking o'er life's finished story,
> Then, Lord, shall I fully know,
> Not till then, how much I owe.
>
> When I stand before the throne,
> Dressed in beauty not my own,
> When I see Thee as Thou art,
> Love Thee with unsinning heart,
> Then, Lord, shall I fully know,
> Not till then, how much I owe.

But in my opinion, we shall not *fully* know it even then. And we shall certainly never be able to describe this salvation as we ought.

THANKS FOR THIS GIFT

Even though the gift of God in Christ is "unspeakable," as the King James Version has it, it is nevertheless to be spoken of. And the primary reason is that it is so indescribable.

To whom shall we speak of it? Well, to God first of all! That is the other half of the text, for 2 Corinthians 9:15 does not speak merely of God's gift. It says, "*Thanks be to God* for his indescribable gift" (emphasis added). Have you thanked God for His great gift of salvation? Have you thanked God for anything? At Christmas you and I thank all kinds of people for more gifts than we probably should have. It is "Thank you for this" and "Thank you for that." But what of God? Is it not wrong and even offensive to be profusely thankful for pens and pencils and CDs and clothes and toys and video games and overlook that one gift that alone is beyond all powers of human description? If that gift is as great as the Bible says it is and as wonderful as our hearts and minds acknowledge it to be, then we should literally cry out with Paul, "Thanks be to God for his indescribable gift!" Thanks be to God for Jesus!

And when we are crying out thanks, let us not forget that the best thanks are not in word alone. Thanks are expressed in deeds, too. What deeds? If you have never received the Lord Jesus Christ as your personal Savior, your first deed should be to receive Him and worship Him, as the shepherds, wise men, and others of the Christmas story did. That is, you should take the gift God gives you. Do not think of it in terms of your worthiness. You are not worthy and never will be worthy. Just take it. Let it be yours. Receive it as that treasure in the field or that pearl of great price for which the wise men and women of this world sell all that they have.

You can also express your thanks by service. You have much, but there are others who have little. Reach out to them in Christ's name. Let God's gift be the pattern for your giving and His service be the pattern for your service.

Finally, know that you are not under obligation to speak only to God about His indescribable gift. You have an obligation to speak to others also. Notice that in the Christmas story nearly everyone spoke to others about God's gift. The wise men said, "We have seen his star in the east and have come to worship him" (Matthew 2:2). The shepherds "spread the word concerning what had been told them about this child" (Luke 2:17). Simeon "praised God" (Luke 2:28). Anna, the prophetess, "gave thanks to God and spoke about the child to all who were looking forward to the redemption of Jerusalem" (Luke 2:38). That last is the perfect combination: thanks to God and testimony to other people.

James Montgomery Boice was senior minister of Tenth Presbyterian Church for thirty years until his death in June 2000. He can still be heard on his international radio broadcast, *The Bible Study Hour*. He was also a prolific author and served for ten years as chairman of the International Council on Biblical Inerrancy.